The Collected Writings of Marcia A. Murphy

The Collected Writings of Marcia A. Murphy

Christus Magnus Medicus Sanat
(Christ, the great physician, heals)

MARCIA A. MURPHY

RESOURCE *Publications* • Eugene, Oregon

THE COLLECTED WRITINGS OF MARCIA A. MURPHY
Christus Magnus Medicus Sanat (Christ, the great physician, heals)

Copyright © 2020 Marcia A. Murphy. All rights reserved. Except for brief quotations in critical publications or reviews, no part of this book may be reproduced in any manner without prior written permission from the publisher. Write: Permissions, Wipf and Stock Publishers, 199 W. 8th Ave., Suite 3, Eugene, OR 97401.

Resource Publications
An Imprint of Wipf and Stock Publishers
199 W. 8th Ave., Suite 3
Eugene, OR 97401

www.wipfandstock.com

PAPERBACK ISBN: 978-1-7252-6197-6
HARDCOVER ISBN: 978-1-7252-6196-9
EBOOK ISBN: 978-1-7252-6198-3

Manufactured in the U.S.A.   03/10/20

Scripture quotations marked (NIV) are taken from the Holy Bible, New International Version®, NIV®. Copyright © 1973, 1978, 1984, 2011 by Biblica, Inc.™ Used by permission of Zondervan. All rights reserved worldwide. www.zondervan.com The "NIV" and "New International Version" are trademarks registered in the United States Patent and Trademark Office by Biblica, Inc.™ Scripture quotations marked ESV are from The Holy Bible, English Standard Version (ESV), copyright ©2001 by Crossway Bibles, a publishing ministry of Good News Publishers. Used by permission. All rights reserved.

Thank you for the permission granted to reprint the following work:

Grand Rounds by Marcia A. Murphy Copyright © (Internet advance access May 4, 2006), 2007, *Schizophrenia Bulletin* 33 no. 3, 657–60. Reproduced by permission of Oxford University Press.

First Person Account: *Meaning in Psychoses* by Marcia A. Murphy Copyright © 1997, *Schizophrenia Bulletin* 23, no. 3 (1997) 541–43. Reproduced by permission of Oxford University Press.

Rejection, Stigma, and Hope by Marcia A. Murphy Copyright © 1998 American Psychological Association. *Psychiatric Rehabilitation Journal* 22, No. 2 (1998) 191–94. Reproduced by permission of the American Psychological Association.

[Coping With] The Spiritual Meaning of Psychosis by Marcia A. Murphy Copyright © 2000 American Psychological Association. *Psychiatric Rehabilitation Journal* 24, No. 2 (2000) 179–83. Reproduced by permission of the American Psychological Association.

Before I Started to Serve by Marcia A. Murphy Copyright © 1998. In *Different Members One Body: Welcoming the Diversity of Abilities in God's Family*, edited by Sharon Kutz-Mellem, 27–28. Louisville: Witherspoon, 1998. Reproduced by permission of Witherspoon Press, Presbyterian Church, (USA).

With love and gratitude to all my fine teachers. God bless you.

When I sit in darkness,
the Lord will be a light to me.
—Micah 7:8b (ESV)

He heals the brokenhearted
and binds up their wounds.
—Psalm 147:3 (ESV)

Contents

Preface ix
Acknowledgments xi
Author's Note xiii

PART I: AN INTEGRATED APPROACH

Grand Rounds 3
First Person Account 14
The Spiritual Meaning of Psychosis 21
Rejection, Stigma, and Hope 31
Psychiatric Illness from the Religious Perspective 38
Before I Started to Serve 44

PART II: COME NOW, LET US REASON TOGETHER

Christian Apologetics & Postmodernism 51
Reflections 61
Letter to My Therapist 65
Eugenics & People with Disabilities 70

PART III: FOR HEALING

Presentation on Spirituality 81
More God, Less Psychiatric Illness 88
Access & Inclusive Mission Handbook 94

Farewell	107
Dawn	117
Bibliography	119

Preface

During my early teen years, I developed a mental illness. Since then my life has taken many turns, some towards recovery. I have written about my experiences so that the lives of others who have a mental illness might be improved. I offer personal insights to stimulate new thought concerning the meaning in psychoses, forces of stigmatization, and how to find hope. My experiences and perspectives have implications not only for the psychiatrically disabled, but also for those who support the ill: their families, therapists, and physicians.

Covering a span of over twenty years these works stimulate new thought, albeit provocative at times, with the aim to reflect a view of the human being that has multiple dimensions which are not always accounted for in the science and practice of psychiatry. Psychiatry, for many years through fits and starts, has stumbled in its attempt to find cures and remedies for mental illness. Such attempts, though heroic in nature, have proven to be incomplete. Antipsychotics have helped patients a great deal but not without diverse, unpleasant, physical disorders resulting from side effects of these medications. Though the psychiatric drugs are all we have been able to offer from the mid-twentieth to early twenty-first century and they have provided some improvement to certain aspects of cognitive functioning and daily life, *emotionally,* many patients are still without hope and resort to substance abuse or even suicide. In this type of milieu, we need to ask ourselves: what else can be done to help the ill? It is my firm conviction that when patients hit rock bottom, they will soon discover the only way out is to look up—yes, up to the heavens; and there, in the source of hope and redemption, is God. We find that we cannot save ourselves.

Preface

So my work has had over the years as its purpose the aim to open doors of spirituality within the psychiatric community and, therefore, the scope of this book through the essays, articles, lectures, and creative nonfiction (story-telling) is to explain what I have learned over the course of my adult life. I do not claim total healing and recovery, nothing so grand as that. But maybe I can offer some insight that would be helpful. And it is through the delicate use of the written language which sits so quietly and passively on the page that I offer a glimpse into that often-sought-after world of faith, healing, and recovery. It quietly sits—waiting—for the reader to possess and to reflect upon.

Christus Magnus Medicus Sanat: Christ, the great physician, heals.

Acknowledgments

There are many people who have supported me over the years giving me the time, strength, and opportunity to write; it would be impossible to name them all. That said, I would like to acknowledge the following gracious individuals and organizations. Those who assisted me in both practical and spiritual ways are Twila Finkelstein, Laura Frey Law, Daniel and Connie Steele, Janis Taylor, Ken and Ginni Gibson, Dave and Marylu Watkins, Richard and Penny Watson, Bruce Walker, Esquire, and his wife, Dedi Walker, Dr. Cecilia Norris, Paul and Margaret Heidger, Myrna Farraj, Rosemary Plapp, Deb Beringer, Mary Richard, Florian Peters, Sarah Dyck, The Reverend Colette Soults, Dr. Paul Meyer and his wife, Peggy Meyer, Dr. Russel Noyes Jr., J.C. Hallman, Maeve Clark, Daniel Stout, and my dear friend, Mary Hubbard. For his excellent work on my book-related author video, I thank Jeff Charis-Carlson for applying his skills and putting in many sacrificial hours.

The Prayer Ministry of Saint Andrew Presbyterian Church, Iowa City, Iowa, have continuously poured out their hearts to God, asking for his blessing and aid for my ministry work and for the many years I spent writing. I am extremely grateful for their generous support. I would like to make special mention of Don and Joan Van Hulzen, dear friends, who, daily, petitioned the Lord to help me in whatever way I needed, in writing, or in my daily life situations, and physical health. I say many thanks for their generosity, and I will always be indebted to them and the entire prayer ministry group.

My deepest and eternal gratitude I lift up to the Lord whom I leaned upon before I was even born. It is God who has sustained me, intervening throughout my entire life with countless miracles and blessings. It is God who gave me the gift of writing and I hope it has always been used for his purposes and glory. Thank you for trusting me with this gift, a broken vessel such as I.

Author's Note

In order to protect the privacy of individuals involved some names, characteristics, and locations have been altered. The exceptions are names of prominent figures and institutions which are known to the public.

PART I

An Integrated Approach

THE RESOURCES IN THIS section are evidence and support for an integrated approach to psychiatric care in treating the body, mind, and spirit. Through my writing I explain how spirituality, alongside of biology and other factors, is an integral part of recovery and is essential for healing the emotional, psychological, and physical suffering inherent in illness. Research has shown that spirituality in particular or, religious faith, play an important role in the recovery process.

Grand Rounds

Schizophrenia Bulletin
Vol. 33, no. 3, (Internet advance access May 4, 2006) (2007) 657–60.

This short story is a work of creative nonfiction and is based on real events from my life. Dr. Gingerich (a pseudonym), my psychiatrist, put on a Grand Rounds on the topic of recovery from schizophrenia. During the Rounds I am interviewed, and I talk to an audience of mainly psychiatric professionals, i.e., medical students, psychiatric residents, and faculty. I give my view of my experience of schizophrenia and what I believe promotes the healing process.

"Would you be willing to be interviewed for Grand Rounds? I'm going to be talking about recovery from schizophrenia, how it is defined, and how frequently it occurs. Partway through my presentation someone else would interview you."

"Yes, I'm willing," I said.

A professor in the School of Medicine at a large midwestern teaching hospital, Dr. Gingerich presented Grand Rounds once a year. He posed this question at one of my regular appointments. Doctor Gingerich was a man of medium build, but was tall and had perfectly neat brown hair. As he sat across from me near a desk, his expression combined the stern look of a disciplinarian and the seriousness of a scholar.

"If it's all right with you, I'd like to prepare some notes beforehand," I said.

"Doctor Chapman, who is Vice Chair for Clinical Affairs of the Psychiatric Department, will be doing the interview. I will ask him for an overview of his proposed questions and get back to you," Dr. Gingerich said.

During the next several weeks I typed up what I might say, and sent it to him.

Doctor Gingerich said it was fine, but I worked on it some more. I changed and lengthened it considerably. I also practiced reading it out loud, speaking into a mini-cassette recorder. Playing it back, I could hear what parts needed work. I wondered how the Rounds would go. My audience would be mainly psychiatrists, psychiatric residents, and medical students who viewed mental illness from the disease (biological) model. Will I be able to communicate my view of recovery? Will I be allowed to say what is important to me? Will they hear and be convinced by my story?

Before the interview I went to the hospital to see what Phillips Auditorium looked like. It was in a newer pavilion that was of modern design. Peering through the open doorway, I saw a podium just right of center and, slightly to its left, a small black table with two chairs in front. There were several hundred seats that slanted upward toward the back and curved inward at the sides.

A few days before the Rounds Dr. Gingerich asked me to be at the auditorium by 10:55 AM on Thursday. He said I could wait in the hallway while he gave my case history.

"When it's time for the interview, someone will tell you to come in. You will sit at the front with Dr. Chapman. I have spoken with him to confirm he will be doing the interview. When speaking, feel free to take as much time as you want. After he has interviewed you, you may leave, and Dr. Chapman will give his perspective and summary. I will then be giving a review of schizophrenia recovery, covering some of the research that is available. I will give you a copy of my presentation."

As the time grew near, I began to feel nervous and was apprehensive about my ability to speak. When I asked an older person I respected for advice, he gave me some needed assurance.

"I think everyone experiences anxiety speaking in front of others, but once you begin, it will lessen. Keep in mind that the people attending the Rounds are interested in you and what you have to say. They are grateful for your willingness to share your experience with them."

It was a cold January morning. I dressed in black slacks with a jacket, and black dress shoes. Living only fifteen minutes from the hospital, I put on my winter coat and headed out. I had picked out a lobby where I might wait and, arriving early, I went over my notes one last time.

I arrived at the auditorium at 10:50 AM. There I sat on a small beige couch and set my backpack on the floor. Medical professionals hurried past on their way into the auditorium, and I recognized a few faces. One was a middle-aged psychiatrist who had spent part of his career at the Community Mental Health Center. Another was a young, curly-haired, bespectacled woman who went by with a spring to her step. Doctor Gingerich arrived just before 11:00. He had on a white lab coat and a navy tie. He smiled, said hello, and held out some papers. I stood, and he explained that after my interview he would give the PowerPoint presentation shown. Within the squares he had definitions of *remission* and *recovery*. He also had data from studies in answer to the question: How frequently does recovery occur? There were also squares showing the long-term course of schizophrenic illness and factors associated with favorable outcome.

"I made copies for you."

He handed them to me.

"Thank you."

"After I review your history, someone will open the door, and ask you to come in,"

Dr. Gingerich reminded me.

"Okay," I said, barely audible.

He left and I waited.

Someone closed the doors, and I heard a deep booming voice over the loudspeaker coming from the auditorium. Though I recognized Dr. Gingerich's authoritative tone, it wasn't loud enough for me to understand. After a while his voice became subdued, and I retreated into my own thoughts. Just answer the questions. What does the audience need to hear? Speak to the needs of the audience.

Then a man opened the door and said, "Come in now."

I walked in avoiding eye contact with the audience, carrying a bottle of water in one hand, and my notes in the other. I had decided beforehand to just look where I was walking and at the people in charge. Doctor Chapman motioned for me to take one of two chairs that faced each other. He asked me to clip on a lapel microphone, which I did. Doctor Chapman had a brisk, businesslike manner. He was of a slender build, and had short black hair, and wide-set eyes. He wore a long-sleeved white shirt and photo ID badge.

After we sat down, he asked, "How have you been doing?"

I froze.

This wasn't a question I had prepared for.

"All right," I said awkwardly, "I do volunteer work."

Hesitating, I didn't know what to say next. I saw in his eyes recognition of my discomfort. He started to ask another question, but at that moment someone from the back row yelled, "We can't hear!"

Doctor Chapman quickly went to the back of the table and adjusted some controls. He then said into his mike, "Test, test. Can you hear it now?"

Scattered around the room voices could be heard.

"Yes, it's okay now."

"We can hear you now."

Doctor Chapman said, "Describe the symptoms that you had in the early stages of your illness and how they affected you."

I immediately glanced at my notes and began.

"When I was in my teens, I was very depressed. I cut my wrists, and then, on one occasion, I overdosed on a bottle of aspirin. I believe this was a reaction to the emotional and physical violence in my home. Needing to get away, after high school I joined a religious cult which operated under the pretense of being Christian but, in reality, was not. At one point, while in my early twenties and staying in New York City, I became psychotic. During the psychotic episode, I heard voices. They began softly, then increased, and became loud. They continued for almost two years. Occasionally, they were affectionate or humorous, but most of the time they were belligerent. Usually, they were disembodied, but sometimes they spoke through things, such as motorcycles, laundry machines, and animals."

I flipped a page to the bottom of the stack. I had put scotch tape across the top corners of the paper to get a better grip.

"On one occasion I heard soft angelic voices like baby angels, and they were soothing. But usually, they used obscenities; they sounded demonic and would mention hell. I felt like I was under assault from another realm, as though evil forces were trying to destroy me. I was terrified, but couldn't communicate that to anyone. And I didn't think anyone could help me. I felt as though I were fighting for my life. At the same time, I was isolated, and felt very lonely. Along with these symptoms, I had long periods of depression and lack of motivation. I was unable to cope with life's problems. I suffered from fatigue, impulsiveness, poor social skills, and listlessness. I was without hope."

Most of the time when not looking at my notes, I looked at Dr. Chapman. At one point, when he raised his hand, I noticed a shiny silver watch. He quickly moved the interview forward with another question.

"What does recovery mean to you?"

As Dr. Chapman spoke I glanced to the left and noticed, for the first time, Dr. Gingerich sitting in the front row. His head was tilted down; he was looking at the floor.

I returned to my notes.

"Recovery can mean many things," I said. "Recovery can be a process, as well as an end. It is not necessarily the disappearance of symptoms, but the attainment of meaningful goals for one's life. Recovery means finding hope and the belief that one may have a better future. It is achieving social reintegration. It is finding a purpose in life and work that is meaningful. Recovery is having clear direction."

Doctor Chapman wanted to keep things rolling; on the edge of my last syllable, he fired: "Give your recovery story."

I saw a few typed words before me.

"After the psychotic episode and hospitalization, I basically went through three stages, the last one leading to recovery. Stage one lasted about eight years. In this stage I had a period of denial, but after I went back for treatment I tried to do what mental health professionals advised me to do: live independently and seek employment. But even though I was cooperative, I could not find my way out of depression and lack of interest in life. I could not find motivation for everyday tasks. I failed numerous attempts at employment and continued to be socially isolated.

"Stage two lasted another eight years. I became disillusioned with psychiatric professionals, and though I continued to see them for medication and counseling, I no longer respected them. I did whatever I wanted to do. I became impulsive, living only for the moment, and this led to foolish choices. I tried a lot of antidepressants, but I was often fatigued, could not set goals, and therefore, could not achieve them. In general, my life was chaotic. I didn't have any direction and lived a self-centered life."

Braving my fears, I glanced up at the audience and thought I saw an old friend I hadn't been in contact with for years. He was now on staff as a computer scientist in brain imaging research.

"I've abused and hurt some people in the past and I'm sorry for that. Stage three began after a near-fatal suicide attempt in 1993. I then began to realize I had a decision to make. It was an intellectual choice, but became a matter of heart. I decided to commit myself to Christ. This decision and the events that followed transformed my life. At this time, I also began a new antipsychotic called Risperdal—"

"Risperdal is a good medication. Maybe your life turned around because you were started on this," Dr. Chapman interjected.

"I agree it's a good drug, but not a cure-all. I have a friend on heavy doses of antipsychotics, including Risperdal, and she still hears voices and has other severe problems. I believe my condition improved because of the combination of Risperdal and my religious faith."

As I looked up to the back row I saw a heavyset resident in green scrubs. He was leaning forward with intensity in his eyes.

"I believe the materialistic view of science and the spiritual view of religion should be integrated. One does not cancel the other; they are different aspects of a single thing. We should end the either/or thinking about this."

"I'm not sure I know what you mean," Dr. Chapman said.

I went on to explain the ideas I had focused on over the past few years. I said that as far as research goes, science is not wrong to pursue biological causes and solutions, yet to ignore the spiritual side of illness is to ignore an important aspect of our experience. It is important for this field to be aware of the positive role faith plays in supporting and facilitating recovery. I then continued my narrative.

"I joined a church and Bible study group. I also began to rise early for Bible reading, prayer, and listening to religious music. This is something I continue to do that helps me to maintain mental and emotional stability. I started to find motivation to do everyday tasks, to set and achieve goals. Only by first placing my trust in God could I then regain my trust in the psychiatric profession and restore my physician to a place of authority. I found others as well, leaders and guides, who gave me valuable advice on how to live. One was Christian writer C. S. Lewis. He said, 'What a sad world it would be with no one to look up to.'"

I had fewer and shorter episodes of depression. There was more joy in life and hope for a better future. I found more opportunities to improve my social skills and I reconciled with my family. Also, changes began when my psychiatrist encouraged me to write. Writing has been an important aspect of my recovery. My interest in integrating medicine and spirituality prompted me to research questions I had. One was, what is the meaning of psychosis? From the scientific, materialist view there seemed to be little meaning in illness. But my faith revealed to me that my illness gives me a chance to glorify God. As a Child of God, I felt my life wasn't worth much unless I could tell others about his kindness and love. Writing has given me a way to do this. I set goals of seeking publication for articles. And my faith gave me the strength to write a book.

"Best-selling author, Anne Lamott, said, 'I don't know much, but I understand how entirely doomed I am without God.' This is also true for me: the only reason I'm alive today is because God intervened."

Doctor Chapman nodded and stood.

"Thank you," he said.

I stood, took off my mike, and handed it to him. After taking my water bottle, I walked across the floor and out of the auditorium. I later heard about Dr. Chapman's summary, Dr. Gingerich's presentation, and the discussion that followed. Doctor Chapman said that he thought I was doing well from a psychiatric standpoint. He felt that my faith had brought me through some difficult times.

After Dr. Gingerich's presentation a gray-haired psychiatrist in the middle row raised his hand.

"How do we know that Marcia's religious faith is not just an extension of her illness, a delusional belief?"

Doctor Gingerich cleared his throat and took a step forward.

"It is true that since Freud's time religion has been viewed as pathology, as fulfillment of a wish for an omnipotent parental figure," he said. "Religion has also been considered a crutch for the weak and feeble-minded. Many have maintained that psychiatry, as a branch of science, must be based on empirical research. And since the existence of God cannot be verified by scientific methods such a belief must be illusionary. However, throughout history, great numbers of people have known a God who has personally revealed himself to them. We should also keep in mind that the founders of modern science, i.e., Copernicus, Kepler, Galileo, and Newton, were men who believed in God.[1] Two who are generally regarded as key figures in the development of scientific methodology, Descartes and Bacon, considered God important.[2] And many of today's scientists are religious men and women as well. To demand that all conform to the philosophy of secular humanism is not right. Mental health professionals must not impose their worldview on patients."

A psychiatric resident raised his hand.

"Marcia is not cured. I'm not sure I understand what you mean by your concept of 'recovery.'"

"In psychiatric terms, we are generally taught that recovery means cure, but that is not the concept that people in the recovery movement have," Dr. Gingerich said. "These people are life-oriented. They see recovery as finding meaning and purpose in life. Instead of focusing on schizophrenia, the disease, they emphasize the potential for growth in the individual. That potential is then developed by integrating medical, psychological, and social interventions."

"I think your terminology is confusing," the resident said.

Several heads nodded in agreement.

"There should be a term besides *recovery* to describe this," the resident insisted.

No one offered any suggestions.

"Are you saying she no longer needs treatment? I don't buy that," the resident said.

"No," Dr. Gingerich said, "I'm not denying illness or saying there is no need for ongoing treatment. I am saying that instead of simply focusing on symptom suppression, the mental health field should focus on the fundamental role of hope, empowerment, and overall wellness of the individual coping with a chronic illness."

A young woman in the front row raised her hand.

"Doctor Gingerich, what are the new treatments and attitudes that are making mental health professionals more optimistic about schizophrenia?"

---

1. Wikipedia, "Life of Christians in Science," Lines 1–45.
2. Wikipedia, "Life of Christians in Science," Lines 1–45.

"That is an excellent question," he said. "Over the past decade it has been the development of the new antipsychotic medications. Other things include cognitive behavioral therapy, social skills training, and new programs in job training. The emphasis on these things varies from country to country. For example, I think that the newer medications have led to the most optimism in the United States. In the United Kingdom and some other parts of Europe, I think it has been cognitive behavioral therapy. Overall, continuing treatment research, both pharmacological and psychosocial, has led to more optimism."

Much discussion followed, and some agreed with the recovery movement's model while others remained skeptical. At the end of the Rounds, the woman with spring in her step approached Dr. Gingerich.

"For Marcia, God's intervention and spiritual healing were clearly important. I feel we need to affirm this with patients who have such beliefs."

Doctor Gingerich nodded, and then an older physician carrying a brown leather briefcase stepped up.

"I think this was the best Grand Rounds in over a year," he said. "It gives me hope for my patients who have schizophrenia. Our previous chairman held the view that no one truly recovers from schizophrenia."

"His opinion was obviously based on a medical model of recovery that stresses cure," Dr. Gingerich said. "According to that model, illness is simply mechanical breakdown or dysfunction."

Several other people told Dr. Gingerich that they also felt it had been one of the best Grand Rounds. Later, in his annual review, the department head told Dr. Gingerich that his Rounds had been well received, and that the ratings for it were the highest on any faculty member for the year. He said he was sorry to have missed it (he had been out of town).

True, my illness had devastated me. It had crushed me in heart, mind, and spirit. The rebuilding of my life took time, twenty-five years in fact. But despite serious illness, I had found meaning. And now, the telling of my story at Grand Rounds had brought glory to God. My illness, in and by itself, appeared to have destroyed me.

But stepping back to see the broader picture, I saw that my painful trial of suffering had had a greater purpose. Though I continue to have setbacks and struggles, I am singing a song of a new and transformed life.

First Person Account

Meaning in Psychoses

Schizophrenia Bulletin
Vol. 23, no. 3, (1997) 542–3.

In First Person Account: Meaning of Psychoses, *I address the scientific community. I encourage mental health professionals to go beyond the biomedical model of brain dysfunction to consider the devastating impact of psychosis. I describe the psychotic symptoms I experienced as a young adult, problems I've had over the years, and factors that led to improvement in my condition.*

First Person Account

For most of my adult life I have existed in a condition considered by doctors to be a mental illness. This illness has been diagnosed as schizophrenia by a competent physician. Since over the years psychiatry has gone through different phases, there have been different theories about the origin of schizophrenia. Most currently adhere to the idea that most serious mental illnesses are brain disorders. It is not currently the fashion in the psychiatric community to search for the meaning of mental illness. The biochemical model of brain dysfunction dominates medical practice at this time and medications are administered with great impact. With the aid of drugs some persons improve dramatically, but there are others who continue to deteriorate. I have found that although psychiatric medication aids in the management of some of my symptoms, it only treats part of the problem.

I believe I have schizophrenia; I have a brain disorder. But along with this biochemical disorder is evidence of another problem. The search for the resolution of this problem has been a healing factor in my life. Not only has the result of this search been healing, but the meaning found through the interpretation of the symptoms has also contributed to a restoration of the self. My search for meaning has shown me errors of interpretation made by others to be what they are—errors.

In this account, I first explain the conditions leading up to my psychotic episode. I describe this experience and other symptoms I've had. Then I discuss the significance of my search for meaning and how it has contributed to improvement in my condition.

During my childhood I was accused of being too sensitive. Before the age of twelve I would get upset fairly often and cry. Then in junior high I became more friendly and outgoing. During this time I was a cheerleader and active in the student government, of which I was elected president. Starting in my freshman year of high school I was on the varsity tennis team. Then in my sophomore year I withdrew from the cheerleaders' squad, not wanting to be in the spotlight. I became very introverted, read a lot of books, and wrote poetry and prose most of the time. I had few friends, and except for being on the tennis team, I withdrew socially. I had more crying spells, cut my wrists with razor blades, and overdosed on aspirin. My parents sent me to a psychiatric nurse for counseling. She and the consulting psychiatrist did not suspect schizophrenia at that time. The first summer after I graduated from high school I was asked if I would like to work out (practice) with certain tennis pros in California. I declined this offer and accepted the invitation to teach tennis instead. I only did this one summer and, soon after, joined a religious group.

The living conditions in this cult were austere. I got very little sleep and put in long days of work. I fasted a few times, once for seven days. I read the Bible or religious materials every day, and prayed often. At one point, I meditated on a single religious phrase all day, repeating it over and over in my mind like a mantra. I had no friends inside the group or out, and I had almost no contact with my family. I lived in a state of poverty and had few possessions. The nutritional value of my food at this time was questionable and there was not much of it.

After about a year of living with this cult, I began to have hallucinations. At first, I thought they were spirits; I thought I heard angels and, later, demons. Upon their arrival I felt no surprise; it seemed natural to me. I was not shocked, but was in awe. What sounded like baby angels was soothing; they sounded sweet and loving. They comforted me. But the demons were chilling and I was terrified. Sometimes I had to go to bed with the light on I was so frightened. The demons mocked and scorned me and sounded menacing. Even though the voices told me to do things, I never did what they said. Sometimes the voices came from machines. A running vacuum cleaner called me filthy names. Laundry machines, air conditioners, cars, and motorcycles all taunted me. The flame on the gas stove also spoke. Sometimes I thought I heard footsteps of huge invisible men following me. When I read a book, the words became audible. And when I walked, my footsteps were words. As the wind blew it whispered messages in my ears.

In the midst of all this disintegration of the world as I had known it, one summer evening when night was falling, crickets began to chirp in four-part harmony. The sound was melodious and wonderful. Another time, as I was taking a walk, I came upon some small trees filled with tiny wrens. All of them twittered, excitedly, in little birdie voices: "I love you, Marcia! I love you!" It was so pretty. Walking through a garden, I heard the bees buzzing as little voices. Once during a storm the rain was falling in a heavy downpour, and the sound of it falling became a voice. It said, "Believe in Jesus Christ and you will be saved."

This message within the rainfall and the call to faith it invoked have been important factors in my recovery. A dramatic improvement in my mental health has resulted from this message. In general, the psychiatric community has been reluctant to acknowledge anything of value in psychotic phenomena, but I know in an experiential way that meaning can sometimes be found in them. I do not discount the validity of the medical model of psychiatric disorders. I am only saying that in conjunction with the biochemical disarray of schizophrenia, there can be something else—something discernible amidst the chaos.

These psychotic phenomena lasted for more than a year, although I never lost complete contact with reality for more than a few minutes at a time. Finally, I realized that I needed a psychiatrist. I was not hospitalized at first, but was treated as an outpatient. Then, within a few weeks I was admitted to a hospital, and there the voices vanished. Since this first hospitalization in 1976, there have been only soft noises, not clear voices, and only intermittently.

I have schizophrenia but this diagnosis covers a broad range of symptoms and many kinds of illness. I have not been paranoid. Beginning at age twenty-two, I had one psychotic episode that lasted about eighteen months—until I sought treatment. I have never again heard a clear voice; the soft noises occur only infrequently and do not annoy or distract me. A few successive hospitalizations have been because of depression. I've needed antidepressants off and on for many years. I've also had many negative symptoms that make it extremely hard to motivate myself or perform any task or job. It has been hard to become interested in anything. Quite often, it has been very difficult to determine whether I am depressed or apathetic, a negative symptom. Whether labeled as negative symptoms or as depression, this lack of interest and motivation has been a major problem for me.

One symptom of schizophrenia is disorganization. It is true that even though I consider myself methodical in nature, my life had been very chaotic up until 1994. I went through twenty paid jobs and six volunteer positions. The longest I was able to stay with a paid job was eighteen months and it was only part-time. As a volunteer, my most successful venture was working at a domestic violence shelter which lasted on and off for four years. My scholarly achievements extended to finishing a year in college and being asked to participate in an honors program. Along with my unstable employment record and short college career, I have been in various relationships, some of which were disastrous.

Many people with schizophrenia have thought disturbances. I do not have this problem. Quite the contrary, a few people have commented that I sound quite rational and do not appear to be ill.

In his book about mental illness, *The Far Side of Madness,* John Weir Perry says that he takes a holistic view of the human being—that the psychic and somatic processes are *indissolubly interwoven.*[1] He believes the best therapy for psychosis considers both the *psychic turmoil and the biochemical reflections of it.*[2] Doctors may think psychoses are the result of physiological disorder because science and religion have long been considered immiscible. So, if someone in the field of psychology or psychiatry does not believe in God or spirituality his or her interpretation of what happens to a person may leave out the possibility that God played a part in or through that person's psychotic experience.

What may be derived from hallucinations? Can they have any meaning? Atheist psychiatrists may not think so and discount such ideas. When a therapist interprets thoughts, feelings, and behavior of his or her client using drug and psychological therapies, he or she may neglect a significant part of the psyche. Perhaps God can work through psychotic phenomena, and perhaps the psychosis of schizophrenia may bring about a fundamental reorganization of the self. The purpose of it may have been to transform my life—for indeed it has.

---

1. Perry, *Far Side of Madness,* 3.
2. Perry, *Far Side of Madness,* 4.

Scientific drug therapy and a life of faith have worked together in my recovery. The drug risperidone is the first antipsychotic that has alleviated my negative symptoms, although nothing has eliminated the soft noises I hear intermittently. Also, risperidone may be giving me more emotional stability. Finding the correct dosage has been difficult, and doctors need to be very careful not to overprescribe. Along with taking this medication I have sought help from my religion. I attend church services and a Bible study class. It is the combination of risperidone and religious practice that gives me clear thinking.

Another improvement is that the extreme impulsiveness of my past has lessened a great deal. A big part of the original cause of that behavior was my own defiant attitude. Having been abused by authority figures in the past, I became disillusioned by people in authority. Therefore, I did not respect such persons or feel a need to obey rules. By turning back to religion, my impulsivity has diminished. I found orderliness in my thinking and respect for authority. The chaos of my schizophrenic behavior is nearly gone for I find I like to obey rules and feel the *anything goes* philosophy I once had is self-destructive.

Once in a while I still have setbacks, but in general, I'm doing much better. I have a lot more motivation and not so many negative symptoms or depression. When I relied only upon medication my condition was still poor. Drugs could only do so much and something was lacking.

For example, I now see that much of my depression was a nihilistic crisis. Nihilism is a general rejection of customary beliefs in morality, religion, and the like. It is the belief that there is no meaning or purpose in existence. This kind of crisis affects many in our materialistic Western culture. I denied the existence of any knowledge or truth. This is something that still creeps into my life almost daily. The problem of not finding meaning made me feel like a boat without a rudder and a ship without a captain. After all, if there is no purpose, why get up in the morning? And if there is no absolute basis for knowledge, why believe anything at all? This was quite depressing! My current belief system has aided me with these problems and I no longer need medication for depression.

Another significant factor in my improvement has been the type of medical treatment and guidance I have received. I am fortunate to have had, for the past twenty years, a psychiatrist who favors a holistic approach to mental illness. I am grateful for the compassionate care I have received. My doctor treats me as more than a biological machine. Much of my good health stems from the fact I have been given support while searching for answers to the complex problem of schizophrenia.

Regardless of whether a therapist is atheistic, agnostic, or theistic, it is helpful when treating a person with schizophrenia to respect his or her belief system. Quite often an ill person may intuitively move in the right direction toward recovery. When doctors consider the belief system of a person they may gain insight into directions to take in psychotherapy and medication adjustment.

If you don't believe there can be meaning in an illness, my story is one that should challenge your thinking. My condition has improved dramatically not only because of finding the right medication, but also because of a change in my belief system prompted by the content of hallucinations. The way I view the illness and the world incorporates both science and religion. I find them quite compatible.

The Spiritual Meaning of Psychosis

Psychiatric Rehabilitation Journal
Vol. 24, no. 2 (2000) 179–83.

In The Spiritual Meaning of Psychosis, *I present a thematic analysis of the meaning of psychosis. This is based on interviews I conducted on individuals who were taking part in a rehabilitation program. In this article I ask the psychiatric community to consider these persons' interpretations of psychotic phenomena. And I urge counselors, therapists, and doctors to recognize how spiritual attitudes and lifestyles give direction and meaning to the lives of those with psychiatric disabilities.*

Special note: When the Psychiatric Rehabilitation Journal originally published this article, their editorial department incorrectly added: "Coping With" to the title. They errored. The correct title is as presented in this current book.

Psychosis can have profound meaning for persons who have experienced it. The meaning attached to psychotic episodes can often be found in the hallucinogenic content of the experience. This article describes themes that emerged from interviews I conducted on eight persons with psychiatric disabilities. I am also a psychiatrically disabled person, but this study focused on the experiences of others, some of whom attend a psychosocial rehabilitation center for the mentally ill called a clubhouse. It is important for those involved with the mentally ill, i.e., the psychiatric community, to consider these themes. They call attention to painful struggles that may occur within the ill person's mind, often involving conflict between life and death. They point to attitudes, behaviors, and beliefs which significantly influence the quality of life for those with psychiatric disabilities. Also, they show that despite the suffering that psychoses cause, meaning may be found that promotes the sanctity of life. These themes have implications both for individuals who experience psychoses and for psychiatric professionals who treat them.

The terms *psychosis, hallucination,* and *mental illness* are derived from the medical model of disease common to mainstream psychiatry. Other models, based on diverse philosophies and world views, attribute psychiatric symptoms to varied origins, some of them supernatural or spiritual. Different models of health and disease do not necessarily invalidate one another, but may focus upon different aspects of an experience.[1] It is beyond the scope of this paper to evaluate different models along with their diverse labeling of mental phenomenon. Instead, I have chosen to use medical terms common to the Western psychiatric community, but the reader should be mindful that other interpretations of psychiatric illness exist. However, this paper's assertion is true regardless of which model is applied. For what I identified as *illness* is actually purposeful in nature and the success or failure of the *psychosis* has to do with universal truths regardless of the therapist's interpretation.

The psychosis—its experiential reality—has proven to have consequences in the daily life of the ill. For example, when voices call a person derogatory names, he or she feels persecuted and

---

1. Tamm, "Different Models of Health," 224.

oppressed. Voices that threaten cause fear. And when they say, "kill yourself," some people follow their command and commit suicide. This means that hallucinations can be persuasive and cause intense emotional reactions that may even result in destruction of life. Therefore, it is wise for psychiatrists, therapists, and counselors to consider the content of hallucinations.

Over the years I have seen heroic efforts made by psychiatric professionals to prevent clubhouse members from committing suicide. A feeling of despair overtakes many people with mental illness causing them to become suicidal. Often death romances them, making darkness look appealing. It seduces some into self-destructive behaviors through a gradual process such as smoking or an abrupt, violent end as in jumping off a tall building. Therefore, whatever gives hope and light to such people is valuable.

In the process of finding members of the clubhouse to interview for this study, I extended an invitation to anyone who had experienced a psychotic episode. No potential participant was excluded on account of his or her belief system or lifestyle. The age at which the eight persons interviewed had their first psychotic episode varied from seven years of age to thirty-five. The educational level completed was: three high school graduates, two with one or more years of college, one college graduate, and two with Master's degrees. There was no relationship between age of onset of hallucinations or educational level and the content of hallucinations. Even though some had experienced delusions, this study's primary focus was on hallucinations. The diagnostic break down of participants was: six with schizophrenia, one with schizo-affective disorder and one with bipolar disorder.

I asked participants about both negative and positive experiences. Some of both were reported. However, most participants emphasized an evil presence during their psychotic episode, while many reported good afterwards.

NATURE OF PSYCHOSES

Beth was in college when she started to withdraw socially and then was hospitalized with her first psychotic episode. She heard frightening voices and felt like she was battling evil. It felt to her as though she were fighting for her life and the lives of her family and friends. She was terrified because she felt as though dark forces were trying to destroy her. She remembers that once, when locked in a quiet room she kept looking for a crucifix. "I needed to see one," she said, "because I was fighting for my life."

Beth also remembers voices saying, "Kill your mother!" Other times they made racist remarks and called people derogatory names. They told Beth she was stupid and no good. The voices used profanity, cursing God, Jesus, and the Holy Spirit. Beth believes her psychosis represented covert warfare.

When Janet first became ill she heard six different voices. One said it was going to kill her. Another told her to kill the mayor, and the rest said a variety of things. At the time, she was attending seminary where the voices helped her write papers. When she received failing grades she rewrote them without using the voices' suggestions. Occasionally, a voice said something positive like, "I love you." Janet said that, for her, the voices were real. From her religious background she knew about Satan and believed they came from him. Janet felt a lot of fear during this time; she thought she was lost to Satan.

Ron was in a psychiatric hospital suffering from depression when he first became psychotic. He was on a low dose of an antidepressant when, suddenly, the staff increased it by four times the original amount. He said this triggered a psychotic episode. Not only did he hear voices—he had visual hallucinations. These were of rough looking men who motioned for him to come, then shook angry fists as though they were going to beat him up. He also had vivid nightmares. One time the voices convinced him that he had killed his brother, which was untrue. He said they sounded malevolent and he felt as though he were in hell.

Linda was only seven years old when she first heard voices. She experienced much abuse as a child. Contributing to the trauma that took place in her home were auditory hallucinations (voices) that told her she was a bad person. Many times the voices told her to kill herself, that she would feel better if she died. They were persistent and became more malicious in her teen years when she began using street drugs and alcohol. The voices' strongest message was that if she committed suicide, she would know God, heaven, and the spirit world. Then she would come back to life. It was told her that if she died, she would learn all the answers and be resurrected. Then her life would be grand. As a result, she almost drank Drano. A counselor helped her get to a hospital before she hurt herself. Only a few times did a voice say something positive, such as, "Life is ok; you're doing ok."

Anne started having psychiatric problems in her thirties after giving birth to her fourth child. She heard voices for about twenty-four hours. One was the voice of a psychiatrist she had seen in the past. He was saying positive things about her to other people. She also heard imaginary airplanes flying over the house and music that changed quickly to match the mood and content of her thoughts. Anne did not report sinister hallucinogenic content; however, she was paranoid during her psychotic episode and believed her phone, house, and car were bugged.

Among the eight participants Sue was unique because when she was psychotic, she hallucinated in all five senses. She identified themes of good and evil. Some of the hallucinations were positive and uplifting, but the majority were negative. When psychotic, she thought there was an evil plot against her and her family. She felt pressure to do or say the right thing, and felt that if she made the slightest mistake, evil people or forces would kill her family, as well as her. She was extremely frightened. When Sue was hospitalized she was afraid to sleep at night for fear someone was going to kill her. At that time, many of the visual hallucinations were of small men. She felt they were wicked people.

Sue also felt there were levels of evil. There seemed to be a malicious presence and something similar to a pattern or maze. In her words, "There was a complicated entanglement that led to another even more evil level. And then this whole pattern would continue, it would go to one more level, and one more level. I think there were only about four levels. But they were extremely scary. Each level was worse and more evil."

Barb was fourteen when she began to hear voices. As she described it, she began to talk to spirits. This frightened her. Also, once, when psychotic, her perception seemed surreal and she wanted to scratch off her face.

Hannah was also fourteen when she began to hear voices, and they filled her with fear. They said they were going to get her. She heard strange talking in her head and these voices often gave her false information. For example, they said that if she did not smoke a cigarette, something bad would happen to her. They called her derogatory names and told her she was a bad person. On one occasion she thought satanic people were at the door of her room.

STRATEGIES FOR SURVIVAL

From these examples it is apparent that psychotic episodes can cause great suffering. The participants felt that dark, sinister forces were at work, sometimes aimed at destroying them and/or their loved ones. Many believed the voices were real. But real or imagined, their influence was felt. And to propound their misery, many had existential crises following their psychotic episodes. They questioned whether there was any meaning in life or purpose to their existence. Such questioning sometimes caused depression, but the participants' religious faith or personal spiritual conviction often provided answers. Some became involved in organized religious communities, while others kept to private, individualized spiritual beliefs and practices.

Some participants found in their belief systems a source of strength to counter dark forces. Their religious faith and practice also fostered attitudes that promoted health and well-being. Such faith may contribute toward progress in psychiatric treatment.[2] Psychiatric professionals—even those who lack religious

---

2. Fallot, "Place of Spirituality and Religion," 9–10; Sullivan, "Recoiling, Regrouping, and Recovering," 28–32.

perspective—need to be aware of this resource and listen to their clients' religious experiences and concerns.

Regardless of a therapist's spiritual beliefs or lack of them, it is prudent for him or her to recognize attitudes and practices that increase mental stability and emotional well-being.[3] For several of those I interviewed, it was their faith in God that kept them from killing themselves. Just as the *evil forces* of psychosis had destructive consequences, good forces of religious beliefs—those that incorporated spiritual reality into personal experience—also had their consequences. By incorporating spiritual reality into personal experience I mean that the person came to view the world and reality with a spiritual perspective. Based on this perspective they focused their attention on spiritual truths, some of which are found in scripture, and participated in activities such as prayer or meditation that connects them to the spiritual Source. Also, for those involved in organized religion, this included church activities. This spiritual awareness and participation empowered them to make positive changes in their lives. The resulting improvement in the participants' mental condition was often substantial and worthy of consideration.

The implications are clear. Those who have suffered from what was for them, evil oppression may find strength to carry on with their lives, often in very productive ways. For example, Beth said that her faith now gives her hope. She believes she survived because of her relationship with a higher power and because people prayed for her. Beth reads the Bible daily, prays, attends Bible study, and church services. She says it is important to be able to discuss her faith with her counselor because it is a big part of her life. It really matters to her.

Ron explained how his faith helped him to get through his psychosis. He says he now has a better attitude and feels better because Jesus is his Savior. He has hope for the future. Ron said religion does not come up much in conversations with psychiatric professionals. He said he has not mentioned his religious beliefs very often because he thinks many psychiatrists and therapists

---

3. Richards and Bergin, *Spiritual Strategy*, 12.

dismiss religious beliefs as delusions—which they are not. He wants to protect himself and keep his faith private. Up until the time of his psychotic episode Ron had been an atheist. He became a Christian after his mental breakdown.

Linda has found that prayer helps her. In her words: "God gives me strength, gives me strength within myself to better myself. Prayer makes me stronger. I pray every morning." Reading the Bible increases her faith and the ability to cope. She said there are passages that apply to her situation, one being, *I can do everything through him who gives me strength*. Phil. 4:13 (NIV). Linda believes God helped her get through the experience of delusions and hallucinations so that she might continue with life. She said that before turning to God she despaired; she didn't think there was anyone out there for her. She says that her faith and religious activity now give her hope.

Sue believes she would not have been able to survive without her faith. She says she would have killed herself. For the most part, her psychiatrists and therapists have been supportive of her relationship with the Lord and of her support system through the church. They have been very encouraging. For a while, she had a therapist who didn't believe in God but felt a spiritual connection through nature. But Sue told her about her activities within the church and her religious perspective and this therapist was supportive of that whole aspect of her life.

However, earlier, Sue had a therapist that didn't approve of her religious practice. This therapist was an atheist and felt that Sue's church, pastor, family, and religious friends had too much influence on her, and that her relationships with them were unhealthy. She thought Sue needed to distance herself from these people and rediscover who she was and what she wanted in life. So the therapist advised Sue to cut off her relationship with God, the church, and her family. The therapist said she was taking Sue apart so as to put her back together and make her a new person. Sue said the therapist succeeded in taking her apart but never put her back together. She said: "I was floundering and lost, and I got in with the wrong kind of people. I started drinking quite a bit, and that was the time I got hooked on smoking." Fortunately, after about six months, Sue started seeing a new therapist, and reestablished her relationship with God and her religious support network.

Sue believes in a holistic approach to mental health that includes the health of mind, spirit, and body. She also believes that a relationship with a higher power is important. She has found her faith compatible with ideas about recovery and mental health. For her, recovery in mental health terms is: living the most satisfying and fulfilling life possible despite having a mental illness.

Even though those who participated in this study saw their faith as important in their recovery, they also stressed the importance of medication. Their religious beliefs did not conflict with drug or psychological therapies.

CONCLUSION

The examples of psychosis given above had strong experiential themes. First of all, these psychotic individuals felt they were under demonic attack. Second, they felt they were bad people because of negative comments made about them. And third, they believed they were in a struggle to survive, to save their own lives or the lives of others. Less often, positive themes emerged, but this occurred infrequently. When hallucinations involved beautiful, encouraging, or supportive content, some found these to have real meaning and considered them to be divine in nature. Still, others believed them to be deceptions on the part of the devil.

When asked what impact psychosis had had and what meaning they had found in illness, more positive themes emerged. For example, Beth responded that her psychosis had made her stronger. She said she has had to fight and struggle for most of her life. But also, the illness has given her a different outlook from most people. She finds herself more accepting of those who are different because of their disabilities, illnesses, etc. She sticks up for people with disabilities when others discriminate against them.

When Sue was asked how her illness had affected her philosophy of life, she replied, "I feel I am a different person because I have had mental illness. It is difficult to say, but after going through all the struggles, trials, and tribulations of coping with a mental illness, I feel I am a better person than I might have been otherwise. I might have been more shallow and superficial. I think I'm more able to empathize with and help other people. And, with my current job I find that I have an opportunity as a mental health advocate to help a lot of people, and that adds a great deal of meaning to my life."

As stated above, both Beth and Sue felt that psychiatric illness had changed their lives in positive ways. Therapy should involve exploration in depth for such beneficial and positive changes that may have taken place and provide encouragement for them to evolve. With proper treatment and support, psychotic episodes have transformative potential.[4]

However, even with the positive life-changing qualities, mental illness can be devastating for those who experience it. It often takes months or even years to recover from a psychosis. The negative effects of a psychotic episode include depression and a loss of will to continue living. A relationship with a higher power may be the only safeguard against suicide. It is increasingly evident that in conjunction with medication, a spiritual life aids the mentally ill. Thus, reliance on the psychiatric community is only one part of the equation, and when the psychiatric professional listens to the spiritual beliefs held by persons with psychiatric disabilities, this aids in the healing process.[5] A client's interpretation of his or her psychotic episode and how to deal with it has relevance. And, often, the solutions they find gives real meaning to their lives.

---

4. Grof, "Human Nature," 345.

5. Richards and Bergin, *Spiritual Stategy,* 9; Sullivan, "Recoiling, Regrouping, and Recovering," 32.

Rejection, Stigma, and Hope

Psychiatric Rehabilitation Journal
Vol. 22, no. 2 (1998) 191–4.

This essay describes the pain caused by stigmatization of the mentally ill. I share my own experience of stigma, as well as the experiences of those at the rehabilitation center where I conducted interviews. I also give examples of discrimination and prejudice. To conclude the article, I tell of how I found hope in the face of rejection, and how I believe mental health professionals and organizations can restore dignity to the lives of those with psychiatric illness.

To have a mental illness in Western society is to be treated as an outcast. Living most of my adult life with schizophrenia, I have felt stigmatization. I would like to share how it feels to have a psychiatric disability and be rejected because of it. Then, I will describe what, for me, proved to be sources of courage and hope.

A little over twenty years ago I had a mental breakdown. Being a naive and vulnerable teenager, I left home and family to join a cult. The rigidly controlled and harsh environment of this cult was like that of a prisoner of war camp where members were brainwashed by means of techniques similar to those used during the Korean War. For me it brought with it the onset of vivid auditory hallucinations and was the beginning of a journey into the psychiatric system—the psychiatric hospital, mental health center, and psychotropic drugs.

Looking back, my biggest struggle was not with the illness itself, but with being tossed aside by the normally functioning world and made an outcast of society. Being treated as less than human because of mental illness sent me into the darkest depression. Nothing compares with being rejected over and over, and treated as if one were a freak, unworthy of respect. No, the psychotic symptoms were not the cause of my despair. It was realizing that because there is no cure for schizophrenia, I must wear this label for the rest of my life, and as a result of it, be considered different and treated as an inferior being.

The world has blamed me for not holding down a job and supporting myself. People said I was lazy because I sat around a lot when I did not feel well. I was apathetic and there was little to inspire me. People felt it was my fault that I was not motivated. I would sleep too much and overeat. Then I would consume large amounts of caffeinated drinks in an attempt to function normally.

At times, trying to communicate with people who spoke too fast was difficult. I was not able to follow their train of thought. And when I was under stress, my words came out jumbled and did not make sense. I wanted to be just like other people who went to college and got a degree. But because of my disability, it was impossible for me to graduate. Often people talk around me and not to me. They do not look me in the eye. I want to tell them I am a human being too.

Rejection, Stigma, and Hope

What is it about people with mental illness that offends the world? Or rather, what does this rejection of people with mental illness say about the society we live in? In the United States, we have a country of great wealth in which many hold a materialistic view. This mind set is one that places high value on the accumulation of goods and the achievement of status. The status of a person is determined by external standards such as his or her wealth, attractive appearance, and academic credentials. So often, people with mental illness are poor, cannot keep up their appearance, and are mentally impaired. This capitalist country stresses competition and reward for achievement. Many of my friends and I with psychiatric disabilities cannot compete, gain status, even survive on our own. I have found that most people want to associate with those who are strong and successful; very few befriend the weak, the damaged, or the broken.

Stigmatization is a way of treating people that indicates to them that they are considered abnormal and substandard. When people with mental illness are ostracized in this manner they often befriend each other, forming a bond. This bond is strengthened by the rejection they experience at the hands of others. Being desperate for love and acceptance we draw close to one another, forming a subculture. It is not based on the values of our materialistic culture, but on love and caring, mutual respect, and cooperation. These attitudes can be found at the rehabilitation center I attend that is associated with our mental health center. It is called the Clubhouse. It provides opportunities for members to socialize and work on specific tasks. Also, there are educational projects that provide opportunities for study. All this is done on a volunteer basis. There I am not judged by external standards. There I find a spirit of cooperation, not competition. At this center I gain a feeling of community that inspires hope. It is an oasis in the desert of a cold world. There I find acceptance. I have contributed to the community by serving as editor of our newsletter. This work was a way for me to get outside of myself, to do something for others and be productive, all in an atmosphere of approval.

Center members have told me stories of discrimination and prejudice. Some of these stories have involved employers and coworkers. One friend said she told her supervisor that she had schizophrenia. Her supervisor then began to act afraid of her, and from that point, often raised her voice in anger and verbally abused her. Another member was harassed by coworkers after they learned that she had depression. They told her that her judgement was not trustworthy because of her condition. Under the circumstances she felt powerless.

Members who have lived in residential facilities have sometimes been treated badly by the staff. One twenty-year-old woman who uses a wheelchair was addressed by a physician as though she were a two year old. At the time, she had been taking college courses. The doctor's voice was sing-songie and condescending. A man at a different facility was denied antidepressant medication and told he should just pull himself out of it. He was extremely depressed and suicidal. This withholding of medication went on for weeks, until he threatened to call the doctor. Only then did they give it to him. Another Clubhouse member had the experience of being on medication that made her laconic. It made it difficult for her to speak and caused substantial weight gain. She felt that her speech difficulties and excessive weight increased prejudice against her.

I was told that once arrangements were being made to go to a restaurant. The manager said they would close the restaurant because the public would not want to eat with those kinds of people. When one member of the Clubhouse went into a convenience store, the manager treated him with contempt. Because of his mental illness he had had difficulty keeping up a neat appearance. He had become overweight, had a scraggly beard, and his clothes were not clean. When the manager gave him his change, she was aggressive, and threw the money into his hand. Whenever he entered the store she refused to speak to him and had a scowl on her face.

Another Clubhouse member told me that he had been ostracized by his family and relatives. When there were family gatherings relatives all talked around him, and only to each other. They did not involve him in their conversations. This made him feel unloved and unwanted. To me this seemed especially tragic, for home and family should be where people find acceptance and support. A basic need is to have someone to talk to. Sometimes relatives will not take the time to talk on the telephone or visit a family member in his or her home. They are often unavailable. The message given is that the person is not worth the relative's time or affection. When relatives neglect a family member, he or she may desperately search for this care outside the family. Friends may become the primary source of emotional support, often providing what the relatives have failed to offer. Another member told me she was severely abused by her relatives because of emotional difficulties. When living at home she did not feel well enough to function normally and could not work. They screamed at her, calling her, *weird, lazy*, and *a loser*. Her mother-in-law even tried to strangle her! Naturally, this made her attempts to gain mental stability more difficult.

I can cite examples of prejudice from my own experience involving coworkers. One occurred when I volunteered at a domestic violence shelter. The director was aware that I had a mental illness because I told her this when I was hired. This information must have been spread around, for I soon found others knew by comments I heard. After I had been working at the shelter for several months, one of the paid staff members abused her position by mistreating workers. I allied myself with those who had been mistreated and spoke up in support of them. This person then said to others behind my back, "She's crazy, you know!" And, in this way she attempted to invalidate my viewpoint.

A second occurred while I was volunteering at a hospital library. I worked with another volunteer, a woman who used a wheelchair. She and I checked books in and out at the main desk. After a few weeks she told me about a problematic work situation in another department where she was a paid employee. With tears falling, she spoke of her dilemma involving a career decision. I listened and tried to comfort her. She said she felt depressed about her situation, and it was then that I told her about my problems. I told her I had a psychiatric disability, called schizophrenia. An aghast look came over her face. I tried to explain what kind of symptoms I had dealt with in an attempt to educate yet another person. But from that moment her attitude became one of contempt. When she looked at me, it was as if she were looking at some sort of strange creature. Even though she was spending her life in a wheelchair, my disability was abhorrent to her. Because of such prejudice Clubhouse members need each other for support and understanding. But I have also found acceptance in the religious community to which I belong. It has been a source of hope and inspiration. I attend a church and an ecumenical Bible study group. Most of the people I encounter there are kind and understanding. Christ, the origin of my religion, was rejected by the world just as people with mental illness have been. He was a friend of the outcasts, and spent time with the poor and downtrodden. His followers try to imitate him by caring for the poor, sick, and oppressed. In contrast to the materialistic culture, my religious community values people with disabilities. They have reached out to me and have shown compassion. There are other people in my church who have psychiatric disabilities, but they remain actively involved. I have followed their examples by volunteering in the office and kitchen. Being able to contribute in this way has given me a sense of belonging. Fellowship within the religious community is also valuable. It allows me to spend time with people who have similar beliefs, and is a way for me to get outside of myself and think about the needs and concerns of others.

I believe the source of the religious community's love and care for the sick is God. Having faith in God has also given me hope. By participating in religious practice, including the disciplines of prayer and meditation, I have gained new strength and a new outlook on life. Granted, I still have problems, but my attitude has become one of optimism. I have found a spiritual dimension of healing. I do not believe God gives up on the hopeless ones. This may be seen in the persistent efforts of the psychiatric clinicians. I began seeing a psychiatrist who has never given up on me. When I had my first appointments, I was especially isolated; I had no friends and relations with my family were strained. It was particularly important at this time that I had someone to talk to. Since then, for over twenty years, he has been an instrument of God's love, providing consistent, reliable treatment. I would like to point out that I have been considered and treated by this doctor as more than a sick person or disease. I have been treated as a whole person which is body, mind and spirit. Even though schizophrenia may be the result of a broken brain (as in the biological model of mental illness), treatment needs to address the meaning or purpose of life. A person's belief system can instill hope.

An integral part of my recovery has been my search and discovery of meaning for my life. This is a philosophical and psychological issue that goes beyond mere chemical imbalances in the brain. In this search, I have developed a new world view. I have struggled throughout my adult years to become conscious of decisions I make that either promote psychological well-being (which affirm life) or undermine my mental health (which I try to avoid). My therapy has included open discussion of ideas and issues pertinent to my view, and beliefs about the world, as well as the administration of medication. When a patient is treated respectfully by a psychiatrist who is empathetic and patient, much of the discrimination by society is counteracted. This is a prerequisite for hope.

Although there is much good in the world and in human beings, much of the inhumane treatment of people with psychiatric disabilities portrays the dark side. People with psychiatric disabilities are regarded as inferior and not worthy to exist. When I have felt this judgment I have felt degraded and worthless. Perhaps as the public learns more about mental illness, fear and hatred will be replaced by understanding. From the care I have received through mental health professionals and the rehabilitation center, I have gained some of the strength needed to cope and survive. It is necessary for people with psychiatric disabilities to have reliable, consistent feedback from others that we do, indeed, deserve a place in this world. And I have found that having a relationship with a religious community feeds a still deeper need, one that goes further than therapy. It is my faith that empowers me to get out of bed every morning and to not give up trying. Although I have an illness and have suffered because of it, rejection and discrimination will not destroy me.

Psychiatric Illness from the Religious Perspective

Web-based publication (1997)
https://www.hopeforrecovery.com/psychiatric-illness-religious-perspective/

This essay was written with the intention of promoting spirituality in medicine. Using a combination of personal account and theory, I describe the transformative impact of psychosis. Standing alone, I feel the biomedical model of psychiatric illness is reductionistic. Instead, I believe a holistic view of mental illness is needed that merges secular psychiatry and religion. This validates the interconnectedness of body, mind, and spirit. I describe how adopting this perspective brought healing to my life.

Psychiatric Illness from the Religious Perspective

> A mighty fortress is our God
> A bulwark never failing
> Our helper He amid the flood
> Of mortal ills prevailing
> For still our ancient foe
> Doth seek to work us woe
> His craft and power are great
> And armed with cruel hate
> On earth is not his equal . . . .
> Martin Luther[1]

There is a great cosmic battle going on and a war being waged for the souls of men. The forces of darkness are pitted against the forces of light. I have encountered the darkness and did not come away unscathed. Wounded and broken, I crawled to the shelter of the church. There I found in God's fortress, protection from the destructive and demonic powers which aim to annihilate my soul. The power of God gave victory, through Jesus, his Son.

I did not always follow Christ. Even though as a child I attended church services with my family, my belief in God and Jesus was superficial. I did not take it to heart. My everyday thoughts and actions were not based on spiritual beliefs. I only thought about Jesus on Sunday mornings. As a teenager I experimented with transcendental meditation because I was disillusioned with my family's materialistic lifestyle. Eight months out of high school I joined a cult. It was not overtly satanic; it appeared Christian, fooling many. Its deceptive leaders brainwashed me into accepting beliefs masquerading as biblical, which instead involved a moneymaking scheme. Nevertheless, I was obsessed with God. And then I began to hear voices.

The scientific community calls my experience a mental illness; therefore, the science of medicine, through psychiatry, focuses on healing my sick brain. I find it encouraging that some medical schools are beginning to teach students about the power of faith in the healing process. This teaching presupposes that humans are spiritual beings and that a spiritual world exists. Future doctors are now being taught to consider the truth of the religious world view. This is particularly helpful when examining mental illnesses—their

---

1. Luther, "Almighty Fortress," in *Presbyterian Hymnal*, 260.

origin, their symptoms, and treatment. It is reductionistic to attribute all causes of mental illness to defective brain chemistry; for as recent scientific literature has shown in the study of schizophrenia, the many years of brain research have not determined the cause of schizophrenia. According to Buchanan and Carpenter *Schizophrenia is a brain disease whose pathophysiology has escaped detection despite intensive investigation . . . despite a century of study, what is wrong with the brain (and where) is not known with exactitude.*[2] And also: *The search for an anatomy of schizophrenia has engendered an enormous, almost indigestible mass of data. In no studies do all patients show the same deviations from control samples. No morphological or microscopic abnormality has been found that is either necessary or sufficient for the diagnosis.*[3]

My experience of mental illness has consisted of a combination of biochemical imbalance in the brain in conjunction with psychological and spiritual factors. I believe brain chemistry is the physiological substrate for spiritual experiences; the two are connected. But the field of psychiatry is dominated by secular humanist theory pertaining to the genesis of mental illness and this materialistic view permeates modern culture. Research is focused solely upon the physical brain. This omits two other components of the psyche. One is the unconscious, which has been the concern of psychologists. The second is the spirit, as described by theologians and religious teachers. The depth psychologist, Jung, saw an intersection of the unconscious and spiritual realms.[4] I believe that when I was in a psychotic state, I was actually in an altered state of consciousness that allowed me to experience a spiritual reality. Even though scientists believe chemicals cause hallucinations they do not know how chemicals in the brain are transformed into what is experienced as a hallucination. The process is unknown.

Western medicine is a mechanistic science to fix the physical body. This is applied to humans even though humans are more than physical beings. The brain is considered as only a physical entity:

2. Buchanan and Carpenter, "Neuroanatomies of Schizophrenia," 367.
3. Stevens, "Anatomy of Schizophrenia," 373.
4. Jung, *Memories*, 304–5.

mind without spirit or soul. When biomedicine neglects the spiritual aspect of man, the resulting treatment options are one dimensional. Drugs are the cure-all.

The Bible has many examples of people hearing voices from the spiritual realm who heard the voice of God. Over the centuries, saints and mystics have heard voices and seen visions. But when ordinary people in the twentieth century state they hear voices from a nonphysical reality they are often labeled insane. They may not be hearing the voice of God and the content may not be religious, but who is to say it isn't communication from the spiritual realm? Since psychiatric drugs often subdue the hallucinations in many psychotic patients, this is proof (researchers say) that the psychosis is simply biochemical.

But even if medications affect the brain chemistry in some, causing voices to decrease, this only shows that chemistry is involved in the spiritual experience: *How do I know that electrical impulses are not God's chosen device for communicating to me a spiritual reality that could not otherwise be known?*[5]

Spiritual experiences have physical changes that accompany them, the two are interrelated. One realm does not exclude the other, but are different aspects of a single thing. The psychophysiology of the mind (and spirit) interacts with the body. My experience of psychosis involved an altered consciousness or mystical state. This included altered brain chemistry as well. I had been spending weeks alone in a room praying and reading religious literature. After this long period of prayer and contemplation, I thought I heard a spirit talking. At first, I heard a whisper, then louder voices. For twenty-four hours a day, for several months, they spoke mostly nonsense, sometimes calling me insulting names or giving me orders. Sometimes the voices were frightening; at other times they were melodious and beautiful. What I now consider a voice from heaven came during a rainstorm. In a heavy downpour, the sound of the rain became a voice. It said, *Believe in Jesus Christ and you will be saved!*

These words were a transforming message that I believe came from God. I did not think this for the first fifteen years of being

---

5. Brand and Yancey, *Fearfully and Wonderfully*, 189.

treated for schizophrenia by the secular psychiatric community, for they persuaded me to believe that, first of all, there is no God. Second, they convinced me that humans are just physical beings and psychiatry is a physical science with doctors as mechanics. And third, that life is meaningless because determinism controls all outcomes (the philosophy of materialism in which there is no free will or spiritual freedom of choice). Fortunately, my intuition told me there was more to my experience than what secular psychiatry would allow me to believe. I began to consider what my life had become since my involvement in the cult and the psychotic episode. As I turned away from religion, my atheistic lifestyle took me down many self-destructive roads. Unbearable hardship resulted from countless wrong decisions. With the downward spiral of failure and the decay of living conditions, I began to sense that the voice of the rain called me to a better life.

The patient may experience states of consciousness that have profound spiritual and transformative impact, including near-death experiences, mystical states, and delirious states associated with alterations of brain chemistry. These events may have a positive impact on the individual, or they may lead to distress. The latter occurrence is especially likely when spiritual encounters are rationalized away with modern scientific theories. Reassurance and legitimization of the experience by a health care provider can be very therapeutic.[6]

When my psychosis was rationalized away by modern scientific theories, this had a negative impact. But when it was interpreted as a spiritual encounter, this had a positive effect upon my life. This encouraged me to turn my mind, heart, and life toward God—seeking God. Then my life took on new meaning. I began to view the world from a religious perspective rather than a materialistic one. From this perspective I saw that there are dark forces in the unseen world that try to destroy what is good. They aim to annihilate God's people. This is clearly manifested in the physical world with wars, terrorism, and violence of all kinds everywhere on earth. Emotional, sexual and verbal abuse permeate our society. Rampant greed and exploitation of the powerless dominates

---

6. Waldfogel, "Spirituality in Medicine," 966.

world economic systems. Within this *culture of death*, individuals self-destruct through the use of alcohol, cigarettes, drugs, and other negative behaviors. These external behaviors are indicative of and, inspired by, philosophies which create destructive value systems. People with negative values exhibit negative behavior, because what one values determines behavior.

God is the source of all goodness and positive values. God is a spiritual being and he uses other spiritual beings to help promote his kingdom. However, there are dark spiritual forces at war with those of good. I encountered this darkness in my psychotic episode. The cult I joined had beliefs similar to Christianity, but different in fundamental ways. Because of this my prayers were not in the name of Jesus Christ, but of the cult's founder and so diverted to dark spiritual powers. These forces responded by surrounding me with spirits aimed at destroying me. Demonic voices threatened me. I was terrorized, but the goodness and love of God broke through with his message of the rain. Years later when I accepted it as truth, I began to turn from a self-destructive path to a Christian one. For example, I began to attend church services finding there a haven amidst an evil world. I found Christian people to be God's people, standing up for what is positive and what promotes life.

The secular world still considers the voices I heard to be hallucinations. Call them what you will, but you will know them by their fruits! If I had followed the voices that told me to destroy myself, I would be dead. Instead, I follow the rain's message to believe in Christ. The fruit of this message is that I am inspired to live a positive lifestyle, and with the support of the religious community I am strengthened. Had I tried to win the battle on my own, I would have been defeated. But with God on my side all is won and I gain eternal life.

I have come to the conclusion that there is no good reason to assume that one is limited only to experiences of measurable, physical things. Nor is there any reason to doubt the validity of one's religious experiences. These experiences deserve consideration, and there are grounds for believing that they point toward God himself.[7]

---

7. Kelsey, *Other Side*, 7.

Before I Started to Serve

In *DIFFERENT MEMBERS ONE BODY*
Welcoming the Diversity of Abilities in God's Family
Louisville, KY: Witherspoon Press (1998) 27–28.

Before I Started to Serve *is an essay published by the Presbyterian Church, (USA). In this one I state what any psychiatrist will tell you, that schizophrenia does not involve split or multiple personalities. This misconception has been fueled by the media and Hollywood. I explain that schizophrenia is a term that covers many kinds of symptoms such as: thought disorder, hallucinations (auditory or visual), delusions, apathy, and withdrawal. A person can have some or all of these, and individual cases vary enormously. This essay also provides examples of activities I undertook in the church which led to fellowship and a sense of well-being. By involving myself in the religious community I found that the love of Christ—through the Christian people—counteracts stigmatization that often breaks the heart and crushes the spirit of those with psychiatric disabilities.*

When we think of disability, we imagine a person who uses a wheelchair, or a cane, or being led by a service dog or communicating with sign language. But many disabilities, although just as severe, are less readily apparent. Mental disabilities are in this category. I have suffered from mental illness and at times have been incapacitated by it; but, generally, I appear normal. My illness, schizophrenia, does not involve split or multiple personalities, as the general public believes. This is a misconception fueled by the mass media and Hollywood movies. Schizophrenia is an umbrella word for many kinds of symptoms, some of which are the following: thought disorder, hallucinations (auditory or visual), delusions, apathy, and withdrawal. A person may have some or all of these; individual cases vary enormously. Medication is often used to control most or at least some of these symptoms with much success.

Some Christians believe that a person need only have a healthy relationship with God to get free of mental illness. Pastors and churches with this belief condemn and ostracize the mentally ill, stating they are to blame for their disease. The causes of mental illness are complex, but include biological, as well as psychological and environmental, factors. Any of these factors or a combination may damage a person, causing severe emotional disorder. I believe some Christian people have a view of severe mental illness that is misinformed. Their harsh judgment of those of us with psychiatric disabilities impedes our recovery and may cause a crisis of faith. In my home church and Bible study group there is an environment that fosters acceptance of those of us who have mental and emotional difficulties.

In 1994, I began attending St. Andrew Presbyterian Church, three blocks from my home. Before I started to serve in various ways there, I requested a Stephen minister. The pew card said, "Need a friend?" And since I did, I filled out the card. The Stephen minister made weekly visits to my home and became a friend I could talk to about religious matters. We had a lot in common, as her daughter had schizophrenia. When I had questions pertaining to spiritual issues, she encouraged me to meet with the pastor. He became very helpful. He had experience counseling persons with mental illness and knew about schizophrenia.

The compassion of the Stephen minister and the pastor gave hope that perhaps I had found a community of believers that would accept me. The secular world stigmatizes those of us with psychiatric disabilities; therefore, I had felt degraded and unworthy. When these church members treated me respectfully, I began to gain a sense of dignity. I began volunteering at the church by participating in the prayer ministry. The coordinator welcomed me with open arms. Eventually, I shared with her that I had a psychiatric disability, but she continued to be friendly and appreciative of my involvement in the group. I wrote a small article on the prayer ministry for the church newsletter at her request. We had lunch together and got to know each other more deeply. However, after a while I found this ministry too difficult, and withdrew from it.

The senior pastor then suggested that I attend an ecumenical women's Bible study that met in my church. This group has been a major healing force for me. After I had attended for a month, I volunteered to prepare coffee and set up the chairs. At first, I was extremely anxious and frightened about the commitment. Learning the task was a challenge. There were times I called the group leader to say I was unable to help that week. Then she would find a substitute, but this happened infrequently. One member, who confided to me that she had bipolar (manic-depressive) disorder, offered to take my place if I felt unable to set up. She also is the person who encouraged me to join the church (I had been attending only as a visitor). Now I have attended the Bible study three and a half years and no longer have trouble with the preparation. I am confident that I will not fail. I increased my involvement by working in the kitchen when there were potlucks. Also, when memorial services with luncheons were held for members of the group at my church, I was asked to bake cookies and to help serve. Once, when there was a potluck, a group member phoned to invite me (for I had missed the weekly meeting). She said, "You don't have to bring anything. Just bring yourself." Her friendship has been steadfast, and she has tried to learn more about my illness. Also, she has sent many greeting cards for various holidays.

The atmosphere of respect and trust at St. Andrew has allowed me to feel comfortable enough to volunteer in a number of ways. I have collated the monthly newsletters and the annual reports. I have served coffee between services before the adult education class. I was, at first, self-conscious and afraid of interacting so closely with the congregation as I poured coffee. After doing this several times, however, I grew accustomed to the task and enjoyed it. A friend asked me to be a greeter with her at worship services. I found this rewarding and I enjoyed shaking hands with dozens of members.

I have described numerous ways in which the church has encouraged me, a person with psychiatric disabilities, to be involved. It has been merciful, as Jesus would be. When the powerful and destructive force of stigmatization breaks the hearts of the mentally ill, the church, as an instrument of God's love, helps them to find fellowship and restoration of human dignity.

PART II

Come Now, Let Us Reason Together

But in your hearts honor Christ the Lord as holy, always being prepared to make a defense to anyone who asks you for a reason for the hope that is in you. 1 PETER 3:15A (ESV)

Christian Apologetics & Postmodernism

A Rebuttal

Web-based publication (2009)
https://www.hopeforrecovery.com/
christian-apologetics-postmodernism-rebuttal/

With this paper I hope to clarify various theological and philosophical positions that divide religious communities. Opposing camps often sit side by side on church pews. When we say we worship God what exactly is the focus of our worship? Can it matter to God as to who or what we think he is? Should it matter to us? This composition is just a brief preliminary sketch of a more complicated debate that I may develop elsewhere.

> *You shall have no other gods before me.*
> EXODUS 20:3 (NIV)

> *So he reasoned in the synagogue*
> *with the Jews and the God-fearing Greeks,*
> *as well as in the marketplace day by day*
> *with those who happened to be there.*
> ACTS 17:17 (NIV)

> *But I tell you that men will have to give account*
> *on the day of judgment for every careless word they have spoken.*
> *For by your words you will be acquitted,*
> *and by your words you will be condemned.*
> MATT 12:36–37 (NIV)

> *Then Jesus came to them and said,*
> *"All authority in heaven and on earth has been given to me."*
> MATT 28:18 (NIV)

There is significant division within the Christian community. On the one hand, there are people who believe that Christ is the one and only mediator between God the Father and all humanity, that he is Lord of the universe and Savior of the world. And on the other, are the Christian relativists who believe Christ is the truth only for those who follow him, and that there are alternative truths and various other gods as represented in the other world religions—which is technically defined as polytheism. However, both sides freely admit that they have an incomplete knowledge of God.

> *We can never have a complete or exhaustive knowledge of who God is . . . That our knowledge of God is partial, however, does not indicate that it is . . . untrue. If we were required to have a comprehensive or* total *understanding of the nature of God before we could be assured that we had a true knowledge of him, we would have to reject Christian theism altogether. Christian theology asserts the incomprehensibility of God, a notion that is not only biblical but philosophical as well. As John Calvin expressed it, the finite cannot grasp the infinite . . . No creature, being finite, no matter the level of its intelligence or scope of its knowledge, could possibly fathom entirely the depth of an infinite being.*

To have an exhaustive or comprehensive understanding of an infinite being, one would have to be infinite....[1]

When the term *Triune God* is used, I am referring to the Christian concept of the Holy Trinity, i.e., God the Father, the Son, and the Holy Spirit; three in one. Those who believe that the Triune God is the only and absolute God dispute the relativist's claim to the simultaneously co-existing gods of polytheism. When the believer claims there is one Creator of the world in which we live and this Creator has revealed himself in revelation (the Holy Bible), the believer is accused of arrogance. When he says the Bible is the authoritative revelation of God given for the purpose of the redemption of all humankind, again, he is accused of arrogance.

> *When one examines the arguments on behalf of universalism [all go to Heaven with or without faith in Christ], one finds them to be of very uneven worth, some objections being little more than ad hominem attacks on particulars. For example, it is frequently asserted that it is arrogant and immoral to hold to any doctrine of religious particularism [i.e., that Jesus is the sole means through which all people can know salvation] because one must then regard all persons who disagree with one's own religion as mistaken. This is an odd objection, since the truth of a position is quite independent of the moral qualities of those who believe it. Even if all Christian particularists were arrogant and immoral, that would do nothing to prove that their view is false. In any case, it is not only incorrect to say that arrogance and immorality are necessary conditions of being a particularist—the Christian particularist may have done all he can to discover the religious truth about reality and humbly embraces Christian faith as an undeserved gift—but, even more fundamentally, those who make such accusations find themselves hoist on their own petard. For the universalist believes that his own view is right and that all those adherents to particularistic religious traditions are wrong. Thus, he himself would be convicted of arrogance*

---

1. Sproul, *Defending Your Faith*, 138–39.

and immorality if he were right that holding to a view with which many others disagree is arrogant and immoral.[2]

How does one know what to believe? What it all comes down to is this: who or what does one claim as one's authority? For a society without authority disintegrates into chaos. If a person says that she believes in the Triune God of which Jesus is a part and, therefore, Christ is her authority, her Lord and Savior, why then would she not believe what Christ says when he states that he is the Way, the Truth, and the Life and no one comes to the Father except through him John 14:6 (NIV)? How can a person say that she believes in Christ, yet not believe Christ's words? That would be a contradiction.

A relativist says that Jesus is the truth only for those who follow him and that mankind can know God in other ways. But truth, by definition, if it is true for one, must be true for all; otherwise, it is not truth. It is then just subjective opinion, whim, or taste. And because of the law of noncontradiction, truth, or knowledge of God, cannot be true only in certain circumstances for it cannot contradict itself, i.e., being true only part of the time.

Believing in contradiction is irrational and a seed for insanity. The law of noncontradiction is a fundamental principle of knowledge that allows for interpretations of propositions necessary for rational living. These propositions are necessary for the survival of human beings and all life on earth. Thomas Aquinas said Christianity is a reasonable faith, one that uses the reasoning of the intellect, and the mind only has the ability to know truth through the light of God's grace. Rationality comes by the grace of God.[3]

I do not limit God's revelation to what is revealed in scripture. One cannot limit God. However, I go along with the Presbyterian Church, USA, denomination's (2009) statement that states that if there is any truth to other world religions it would lay in their ability to point the way to Christ.[4] Only in the measure of any of their teachings pointing to Christ as Savior of the world do they hold any

---

2. Moreland and Craig, *Philosophical Foundations*, 617–18.
3. Williams, "Philosophy in the Middle Ages," (Audio Recording).
4. Pcusa.org. (2009).

truth. Jesus Christ has unique authority as Lord and every other authority is finally subject to Christ. At the same time, Presbyterians acknowledge that no one can know all of truth or all of God. Since God is infinite and is of infinite depth, it only follows that it is beyond our limited human capacity to comprehend all of God and his truth.

So it comes back to deciding who or what is one's authority. If a person doesn't look up to anything or anyone above himself, he is deifying himself, making a god or idol of himself. He ends up worshipping himself, which is, indeed, arrogance. If a person venerates philosophies or theologies other than those given by God, this is idol worship.

If a person says the Bible is their authority and it points to Christ, then, again, it would logically follow to believe what Christ says. For a person cannot say *Jesus is Lord*, and then not believe his words. You can't have it both ways. To say that Christ is a great moral teacher but also a liar when stating that he is the only way to the Father is self-contradictory and nonsensical.

Often, Christ is sacrificed in the name of religious pluralism masquerading under the concept of *inclusion*. While it is of paramount importance to be socially inclusive, to treat all humans from all cultures and races with the utmost love, acceptance, and respect, this is not to say they are to be idolized in the sense of being placed above the Triune God. To do so is to deify humans. I strongly believe in inclusion, in loving and accepting all people, but not at the expense of sacrificing Christ's central position in the universe. The Bible says that loving God should come first, then, your neighbor:

Hearing that Jesus had silenced the Sadducees, the Pharisees got together. One of them, an expert in the law, tested him with this question: "Teacher, which is the greatest commandment in the Law?" Jesus replied: "'Love the Lord your God with all your heart and with all your soul and with all your mind.' This is the first and greatest commandment. And the second is like it: 'Love your neighbor as yourself.' All the Law and the Prophets hang on these two commandments." Matt 22: 34–40 (NIV)

In our current situation, in the postmodernist (and New Age) mind, God is not the God of the Bible, but is one that consists in a plurality of choices. In this religious grocery store, gods can be a rock, or a tree, or a cow. God can be an impersonal energy or force, without personality, feelings or intellect. Such a god does not make any demands. It does not require a human's self-denial.

Postmodernist/New Age gods can also be idols of self-fulfillment, self-promotion, and accomplishment. They can be gods of pleasure and hedonism. With such, there is no need of atonement for sin; indeed, there is no acknowledgement of sin. When there is a need for salvation in postmodernist thought, people are saved by works or their own efforts (which is impossible) if the concept of sin is real to them; but for many, it is not. If Jesus' crucifixion and death were necessary only for the salvation of those who follow him, while others find other ways to God—then he died in vain and this makes a mockery of the cross.

Socially, we see a pluralistic society and global community but this pluralism should not carry over into the world of spiritual truth:

> As we confess Jesus as Lord in a plural society, and as the church grows through the coming of people from many different cultural and religious traditions to faith in Christ, we are enabled to learn more of the length and breath and height and depth of the love of God Eph. 3:14-19 (NIV) than we can in a monochrome society. But we must reject the ideology of pluralism. We must reject the invitation to live in a society where everything is subjective and relative, a society which has abandoned the belief that truth can be known and has settled for a purely subjective view of truth—truth for you, but not truth for all . . . In a pluralist society there is always the temptation to judge the importance of any statement of the truth by the number of people who believe it. Truth, for practical purposes, is what most people believe. Christians can fall into this trap . . . .[5]

So, again, it comes down to choices: who or what is our authority? And to whom or what will we bow? A person can pray and ask God if he exists and in what form. She can also ask if the Bible is God's revelation as well as whether Jesus' words are true. Contrary to accusations of an arrogant heart, it may take some humility and

---

5. Newbigin, *Gospel in a Pluralist Society*, 244.

a humble attitude to submit oneself to someone or something beyond oneself and, in doing so, to admit to one's own insufficiency. Saint Augustine, a great philosopher and theologian of the Middle Ages, was a strong proponent of submission to authority, particularly, divine authority.[6] Without daily submission, such a mind-set results in the self-appointed lordship of oneself.

When I heard the following statement: *Jesus Christ is the ultimate truth for those who call him Lord,* it was not clear to me how I should interpret this or what the meaning was. A possible interpretation was: Jesus Christ is the ultimate truth for those who call him Lord, but not for others; they have their own *truths*. In other words, it may have meant: *People who follow Christ believe he is the ultimate truth, while those who do not follow Christ do not believe he is the ultimate truth with no detrimental consequences as a result of their unbelief.*

I believe that Christ is Lord and the ultimate truth for those who call him Lord; and for those who do not choose to call him Lord, he still remains the ultimate truth to which all will be held accountable.

Problems arise when it comes to defining the term *truth*. In many ways, truth, in contemporary society, has lost its meaning. For truth has become synonymous with individual tastes and preferences when, by definition, it actually means that which transcends cultures, times, and places. Truth is foundational and is based within a metaphysical context which has as its source an absolute objective reality independent of time and space and human subjectivity. Truth means, by definition, that if it is true for one, it is true for all.

Josh McDowell and Thomas Williams have written:

If everyone's truth is equally valid, then truth is a meaningless term. A word that can mean anything really means nothing.[7]

To state as truth that Jesus is Lord only for his followers and people of other religions have their own truth about the reality of God is to render *truth* arbitrary and relative. This nullifies the very concept.

---

6. Williams, "Philosophy in the Middle Ages," (Audio Recording).
7. McDowell and Williams, *Search of Certainty*, 34.

In response to atheists, New Agers, postmodernists, relativists, and supporters of the simultaneously existing model of world religions, I'll again, quote McDowell & Williams:

When they claim there are no absolutes, they must believe that this claim, at least, is absolute. And at the very least they must believe their thinking is true when it leads them to conclude that there is no truth. And they must find some way to live with the convoluted inconsistency of such a conclusion . . . .[8]

And author, R. C. Sproul, maintains:

Ironically, no one can be a consistent relativist for very long; even when absolute truth is denied to exist, those denying it affirm at least one absolute, namely, that no absolutes exist.[9]

Some say that scripture is God's word to them and the authoritative witness to Jesus Christ. I believe that the innumerable ways we may come to know Christ are mysterious and ultimately up to God. If one accepts Christ as Lord and scripture as Christ's authoritative witness, it follows that one believes what scripture quotes Christ as saying. Again, to not believe his words would be a contradiction.

Some say that Jesus is Lord and the ultimate truth and that every other kind of truth is penultimate. Penultimate is a term which refers to something that is secondary to or that coexists with something else while retaining its validity. In considering the validity of various religious truth claims and whether or not they can coexist, one cannot throw reason out the window. For example, when making decisions and judgments regarding the material world, logic is demanded. One should also be rational in spiritual matters.

When the truth claims of diverse religions contradict or negate one another it would logically follow that one is true and the other is false. God is a God of reason and rationality, of logic and noncontradiction. Just as there are laws in the empirical world of science, so are there foundational and necessary spiritual, philosophical, and intellectual laws upon which sanity is based. Kenneth Richard Samples explains about one such law that I mentioned before—that of noncontradiction, i.e., A cannot equal A and non-A at the same

---

8. McDowell and Williams, *Search of Certainty*, 68–69.
9. Sproul, *Defending Your Faith*, 35.

time. Jesus Christ cannot be both God incarnate (Christianity) and not-God incarnate (other religions) at the same time.[10]

In a similar vein, if we, as Christians, define God as the Holy Trinity, then something claiming God to be less than this would be a contradiction. Any religion that does not acknowledge Jesus as Lord and the second person of the Trinity cannot be considered the whole truth. Definitions of God are at stake.

One might counter with: *But God is beyond definition!*

While it is true that no human has a complete knowledge of God, I believe that God has revealed himself in scripture. Much of the New Testament is historically verifiable and is, therefore, trustworthy testimony. Any belief, philosophy, or theology that contradicts these doctrines would be is less than penultimate, they would be contradictory. If Christ is, indeed, the only way to the Father, any other claim to knowing God is also less than penultimate—it also becomes contradictory. The law of noncontradiction states that Christ cannot be both the Way and not the Way. And since Islam, Hinduism, and Buddhism (an atheistic religion), all deny the divinity of Christ it follows that Christianity and other religions cannot be true simultaneously.

Jesus was a Jew, and within Judaism and the Hebrew scriptures we see these chosen people in a holy covenant with God that precedes the New Testament years and then extends beyond in some mysterious fashion. The Hebrew scriptures, the Old Testament, through the prophets, and others, point to Christ.

I maintain and, humbly submit, that Christ is Lord in the sense that this is an ultimate absolute truth which is an objective reality transcending all cultures, times, and places. There is but one Creator which is the Triune God—the Holy Trinity. When a Christian relativist says that God is anything you wish God to be, this is stepping outside the bounds of historically verified Christianity. When anything other than the doctrine of the Trinity is postulated as truth this becomes an attempt to deny the validity of Christ's spoken Word. The truth may not be politically correct or popular;

---

10. Samples, *Without a Doubt*, 164.

but there it is. Truth is not determined by our wishful thinking or by society in general.

For there is one God and one mediator between God and men, the man Christ Jesus, who gave himself as a ransom for all men.
1 Timothy 2:5-6a (NIV)

Reflections

Web-based publication (2013)
https://www.hopeforrecovery.com/reflections/

What is the church? Who are God's people? This essay contains my reflections upon the apathetic condition of many who profess Christ. What does the Bible show God to be in regard to the afflicted, poor and oppressed? And, is the Christian community reflecting this God of the Bible and the example of Jesus Christ?

> *We will have to repent in this generation not merely for the vitriolic words and actions of the bad people but for the appalling silence of the good people.*
> MARTIN LUTHER KING JR.
> Letter from the Birmingham Jail[1]

I have a mental illness. The reason I quote MLK Jr., is because the mentally ill have a lot in common with the African-American population. Not only have we faced rejection and discrimination, we are also among those most incarcerated compared to the general population and who are more likely to live at the subsistence level. I will not attempt to go the full depth of what blacks have experienced here—I could not do it justice. I will just begin this essay by saying that the reader should be mindful that mental illness has as a stigmatized illness, much in common with people of other marginalized groups, and because of this we can learn from others how to cope, organize, and move forward.

Too many white, church-going, middle-class Americans are satisfied with the status quo. Content to focus on everyday needs of family and friends, few concern themselves with problems of the oppressed—in this case, the mentally ill—unless, of course, it strikes close to home. Many saturate themselves with entertainments, escapism, and diversions with which to be inoculated from the very real pain of the afflicted. But the God of the Bible and, the example of Jesus Christ, shows that God is deeply concerned for the afflicted, oppressed, poor, and outcast. So it follows that God's people will reflect this biblical God of justice in showing compassion for the poor, sick, and downtrodden. God's people stand up for justice; the Christian church will reflect this merciful God in attitudes and actions. The God of the Bible is not concerned with acquiring wealth or fine palaces; the authentic Christian church will keep its focus not on riches and external appearances, but on the deep inner values of caring for others and helping those in need. You might say that the mentally ill and others similarly afflicted, represent a challenge and litmus test for the Christian community which will reveal who are truly God's people and who are the imposters.

---

1. King Jr., *Letter from the Birmingham Jail*, 18.

Reflections

I have prayed for my mentally ill friends. I have asked God, now, to extend His grace as never before in history. Jesus, who is the Judge and yet, the Defender, must come to our aid. We all need the grace of God.

Reinhold Niebuhr, one of the greatest thinkers of the twentieth century, spoke of the great modern pessimism in perspectives on the state of humanity. A summary of his thought pertaining to this is that he expressed the futility in trying to excuse the vast depravity within man. Yet, he also said that man has a great capacity for justice and it is the duty of a people to work for change and to not give up hope. Niebuhr is a man who witnessed both the first and second World Wars during his lifetime whereby prohibiting him from any trace of naïveté. Yet, when someone expressed the futility in attempting to improve the human condition, he still encouraged action and positive thought in the cause of justice. As a Christian theologian and philosopher, his point was that even in the face of evil humans must work for the good and never give up hope.[2] I, personally, would challenge anyone who states that things never improve. History has proven this otherwise as we see in women's suffrage, civil rights, and even medical care.

For too long the mentally ill have suffered in silence. I came upon the following quote by Simone Weil:

The afflicted are not listened to. They are like someone whose tongue has been cut out and who occasionally forgets the fact. When they move their lips no ear perceives any sound. And they themselves soon sink into impotence in the use of language, because of the certainty of not being heard.[3]

From the mid-1800s to the 1950s, American mental institutions were houses of horror. Though many attempted to help the ill, treatments were few or nonexistent. The mentally ill were warehoused. Many were abandoned. Now in the present day I see that there are some people at the church I attend who would like to help with this cause. I hope that other churches across this country will also take steps to aid the mentally ill in their communities. Again,

---

2. Robertson, *Love and Justice.*
3. Weil, "Human Personality," In *Selected Essays 1934–1943*, 28.

I pray for the grace of God to extend to all that suffer from the affliction of mental illness and that healing will result in furthering the integration of this population into our Christian worship and fellowship.

Letter to My Therapist

In Fact, Fiction, and Little White Lies

The University Club Writers of Iowa City No. 3
Cedar Rapids: Eagle Book Bindery, (2014) 115–17.

Originally written (2013) because of a request from a person putting on a graduate school symposium on the topic of suicide, I wrote this letter to show the depths of problems that may compel a person toward suicidal thoughts and actions. These thoughts are my own, taken from my own experience. The answer from the therapist is authentic—my own therapist responded.

Dear Therapist,

I write this letter because there have been recent criticisms regarding my depressed state to the point of being verbally chastised for my recent suicidal gestures that took me to the emergency room of our university hospital. Not condemnation coming from yourself; but a harsh rebuke by an MD. Your position as a psychologist may give you a more insightful perspective and, hopefully, a more compassionate frame of mind than what I've previously encountered from your insensitive colleague.

As a person with mental illness, having the diagnosis of schizophrenia, I've come face to face with rejection from our society. Being treated as someone inferior, deviant, and unworthy of respect has caused an internalization of these pejoratives that has left me with little or nothing to base a positive sense of self on.

For example, the government's view is to let the mentally ill starve to death which is made evident by the scant monetary benefits provided for me and my fellow disabled friends. Along with that, affordable housing is almost non-existent so not only am I constantly mindful of possible homelessness and death by exposure; when I do find housing, it is most certainly substandard: apartments filled with bugs, air conditioners periodically on the blink; violent, dangerous and predatory neighbors.

Our governor would rather put the mentally ill in prison than give them the psychiatric services they need to get well. He has cut essential programs and terminated residential care facilities which will end in certain death for some of the clients. In a way, this is government-sanctioned murder reminiscent of the Aktion T-4 program of Nazi Germany where all the undesirables and those with no economic value were exterminated. We just have another name for it now: budget cuts. Oh, the money is there. The state has a surplus this year [2013] and, yet, the Governor has the gall to cut important funding which would help the most vulnerable and needy of our society. Then he goes on to say that he wants our state to be number one in health! Now I ask you, how can a population be healthy without their mental health? That comes first.

So you would ask, what have I been depressed about? Why would I want to end my life? Don't I have anything to live for? "Be

Joyful!!," my pastor recently demanded during a church service, then proceeded to lead us in the Christmas song, Joy to the World! (in February).

I'm tired of the way people treat the mentally ill who not only live in poverty and severe deprivation but social ostracization: often being denied medical and dental care; shunned by neighbors, social groups, and relatives; gossiped about behind our backs by co-workers, being openly mocked and ridiculed by those same co-workers; denied service in restaurants, feared by many.

Too long have I wondered where my next meal will come from starting at the middle of each month, trying to find a way to a food bank. Too long have I tried to get rides to church, begging members to help me out each and every week. Too long have I suffered the isolation of an outcast: weekends and nights alone—angry at God and humanity. Why not just walk over to my dresser top and take the prescription bottle? Take it to my table by the chair, counting the tablets—yes, there would be enough. Poor a glass of water, sit down.

It's just one arm motion away—escaping into the deep darkness, perhaps an end to pain. But what if I don't succeed? Need I keep my apartment door unlocked to allow the paramedics easy access? Will there be an odor? Most certainly, after only a few hours. Who would find me? Maybe it's too gross. A dead body is not a pretty thing. It would be embarrassing.

So, let's put the cap back on. Let's put the bottle back on top of the dresser, perhaps until another day or night. Another day or night when I long for a companion, someone to talk to and to whom I can listen, as I longed last night, and the night before, and the one before that. Still, there is no one. Another night when my faith falters and my convictions are shattered. The Bible says that God will provide for all our needs—with the qualifier that we are seeking God's kingdom. I have tried to do this and still hunger. Where is the answer to God's promise? Some say it will come, eventually; perhaps not in our lifetime. In other words, in the afterlife. So I might as well die. Heaven will be a place of loved ones, friends, etc., so why not just do it? End my misery and find happiness and bliss?

There must be a reason I have kept putting the prescription bottle lid back on and carried it back to the dresser. When in the coldest and blackest winter night, when all the demonic underworld surrounds me and beckons to join them, there must have been a tiny wish in my heart to stay on this side of eternity for just a little longer. Maybe, just maybe, things will get better. And that God who seems so aloof now and, to me, evasive, might one day make it radically clear that his purpose for me and my life will supersede and nullify the abundant desperation, hopelessness, and despair I have encountered for so many years. I will trust in this God—again.

SINCERELY, AND WITH THE HIGHEST REGARD,
MARCIA

Answer from the therapist:

MARCIA,

I just read your letter. Your question in the letter is one of hope. Where does one get hope in the face of injustice, loneliness, financial struggles, and emotional difficulties? I can only tell you where I have gotten hope in the toughest times in my own life.

First, hope comes from connections to others. Even when we are lonely and isolated, it is possible, and necessary, to make contact with others. Even when the depth of contact is not all that we wish it were, it is contact. That is why service to others through volunteer activities or work, church or synagogue involvement, friendships, civic activities, clubs, are so important and so sustaining.

Hope comes from spiritual connections, by which I mean a sense that one is connected to other living beings, throughout time and space. Those connections can be fostered by involvement in spiritual communities, books, teachers, communing with nature. There are many doorways into a spiritual life. We have to be willing, and we have to have the strength and curiosity to open the doors and walk in.

Last, for me, hope and determination come from my ancestors. I am Jewish; hope and tenacity have sustained my own people for thousands of years. The best example I can think of is the Austrian/

Jewish psychiatrist Viktor Frankl. He was sent to Auschwitz during World War II. His wife died in another camp. But he did not know until after the war that she had perished. Hope kept Frankl going. However, there is one thing that he did that inspires me in the darkest times: he was a doctor. In Auschwitz there was a sick ward. At the end of the war there was an outbreak of typhus in the camp. As the Germans were finally fleeing, with the Russian army about to liberate Auschwitz, Frankl considered fleeing the camp, too. He was finally free. A patient with typhus asked Frankl if he was going to leave the camp, abandoning the sick prisoners to whatever fate they faced. Frankl decided that he was a doctor, and that no matter what, he must stay and help his patients, putting off his own liberation from Auschwitz.

That gives me hope no matter what. If Viktor Frankl could find hope in that situation, so can we.

REGARDS, DR. T

Eugenics & People with Disabilities

The Roots of Societal Rejection, Neglect, and Indifference

Web-based publication (2013)
https://www.hopeforrecovery.com/
eugenics-people-disabilities-roots-societal-rejection-neglect-indifference/

Who can decide who is worthy of life or death? How do we judge a human being's worth? How do we treat those that society sees as weak and dependent? What is the Christian response? What is yours?

Eugenics & People with Disabilities

To begin, there seems to be a long history of societal neglect and indifference on the part of our culture concerning the plight of the mentally ill.[1] So why am I writing about this issue now? It is because this is still a very urgent problem that some would say is even desperate in nature. I asked an expert in the field of psychiatry at the University of Iowa if there was an urgent need for more community centers and hospital services to care for and treat people with mental illness. I asked if the biggest obstacle in mental health care is the inaccessibility of the system for the majority of the mentally ill. The professor replied: *I'm not sure if it is the majority; but it is a large number and a very real and extremely important issue.*[2]

What has caused this inaccessibility of the system? I am of the opinion that the amount of services for the mentally ill throughout history and what currently is available is a reflection upon the societal values and, subsequently, attitudes towards those who have a psychiatric illness or disability. In biblical times it was the leper who was the outcast. And now in modern times it has been my experience that the mentally ill are, to many, the *undesirables* of our Western culture. To suffer from this disability, as I do, one is placed at the mercy of the able-bodied and strong-minded.

The Judeo-Christian religion, the religious tradition I was brought up in, supports the notion of compassion for the weak and sick and, currently in modern-day America, there are some people, such as many in the health care industry, which uphold a type of dignity of life philosophy for human beings. However, had I lived in Nazi Germany from 1939 into the late 1940s my life would most likely have been cut short. It would have been ended by the Nazi regime which had recruited top academics, as well as, the most revered physicians and nurses of their health care industry to carry out extermination programs.[3]

It may help to clarify my position by use of polarity or contrast. So I will explain. Starting with the eugenics movement in the United States in the early 1900s, a movement to cosmetically

---

1. Pietikainen, *Madness*, 92–93.
2. Psychiatric professional, email message to author, January 4, 2012.
3. Mostert, "Useless Eaters," 155.

harness the reproduction of human beings with the aim of creating the best genetic outcome, it soon made its way across the ocean to Germany. There eugenics was adopted in the attempt to cleanse the German society of the weak and the undesirables: those considered to be inferior, the useless eaters, those who had a physical, emotional, or mental disability. I learned in my studies that this was clearly the aim in the Nazi Germany period of time when the political leaders instigated the Aktion T4 program. In order to establish what they labeled the superior race, Germany murdered over 100,000 disabled babies, children, adults, and elderly by lethal injection, gassing, or starvation.[4]

One would wonder what kind of society could commit such heinous acts. What are the attitudes and values of a people that would allow and even aggressively pursue extermination of the most weak and vulnerable of its citizens? The depravity knew no bounds. In my studies I found that the homogeneity of the German political structure at this time in history encouraged public conformity. So when Hitler rose to power there was little opposition for him. He demanded allegiance backed by a special police force that terrorized the common people. Few had the courage to resist, but some members of the Roman Catholic church, as well as some Lutherans, protested, risking and, for some, losing their lives.[5]

The other side: How do people with disabilities feel?

I decided I wanted to hear from people on the other side, those whom today are cared for by loved ones or supported by government benefits and programs here in the United States because of a disability. So, first, I approached two friends that I had met while volunteering at a hospital in the city where I live. I wanted to know if my handicapped friend and her caretaker think that life has any value for them. Do they experience a meaningful existence? Do their lives have any worth?

[I am using pseudonyms]

Claire, the mother and caretaker, is a slender, red-haired sixty-some year old articulate woman of Irish decent. She loves to talk

---

4. Mostert, "Useless Eaters," 155.
5. Anonymous history professor, personal communication, 2011.

and can gaily converse about almost any topic with intelligence. She can be seen pushing Michelle in her wheelchair around the hospital while they are volunteering. Sometimes, if you look closely into her face, you may see a reflection of a heavy heart. Michelle is Claire's daughter and is a striking beauty with full thick and naturally wavy blond hair. She has a gentle smile and her facial features out shine New York's highest paid fashion models though her speech is labored and it is an effort for her to get the words out. She has limited use of her thin arms and hands and must always rely on her mother's pushing the wheelchair for mobility except when she is driving their pony cart on the farm.

Though Michelle does not suffer from a mental illness I can see a similarity between her kind of disability and those with a mental illness in the sense of having a limited capacity of brain function as well as being dependent upon able-bodied people for survival.

I asked Claire to look over a list of questions I composed. I said, "Claire, here is my list of questions. Feel free to disregard any you are not happy with. Thanks!"

1. Are you familiar with the program called Aktion T4 that was instigated by Nazi Germany before and into the Holocaust where the physically, emotionally, and mentally disabled where systematically murdered by the medical profession? These victims were babies, children, adults, and the elderly. The families often put their loved ones who had a disability into institutions unaware that they would be warehoused. Then the relatives received a fake death certificate stating a fake disease as a cause of death for their loved one. The Aktion T4 program actually got its start when some mothers or fathers had requested the killing of their disabled baby or relative.

    The Nazis wanted to create a master race and wanted to get rid of the weak, inferior people, what they called: Useless Eaters. If people could not work then they were of no economic value to the German system. So the German authorities based their decisions of whether or not to kill the disabled on whether or not the people could work. What is your reaction to this program and what it stood for? What would you have done if you lived in Nazi Germany when this program was being instigated? If this is too strong a question, just any general impression would suffice. What do you think of the attitudes toward the disabled that this program represents?

Claire answered: *I think that system was emotionally cold. I wonder if the people responsible for originating that system considered what would happen to themselves when they reached the point they were thought to be too old or if one of the Nazis had an acquired disabling condition would they too be killed?*

Since I did not live in Nazi Germany it's not possible to know what I would have done for sure, but I believe I would have tried to discourage that kind of thinking and act in as strong a way as I could have; or possibly the only other thing would have been to get away from there.

To me it seems that program represents a fear within those who invented it. That fear being: they themselves were not perfect and they feared being ousted from "the group" so they invented a group of "others" to insure their own standing in the group.

2. How did Michelle become disabled? *Traumatic brain injury from an air embolus in her circulatory system.* At what age? And what is her current age? *Michelle became disabled at twelve years of age. She is currently forty years old.* Has her level of disability increased, lessened, or remained about the same? *Well, her recovery phase took a very long time, probably about one and a half years, and her disability leveled to what she is at right now.*

3. How do you feel as her care provider? *I'm very comfortable and very happy to be her care provider.* What rewards are there? *I have had many rewards. Still having her as part of the family is the biggest one.* What does Michelle have to offer to the world and why is the world a better place because she is here? *She motivates people, makes them feel appreciated, isn't confrontational or threatening so people feel safe. She shares her*

sense of humor and is sensitive to others' feelings. She sets a good example for others to know how to care about people.

4. Do you feel/think that Michelle has a meaningful life? *Yes.* Also, what joys and sorrows does she experience? *I believe she is like most other people in those areas—it's more joyful for her when she knows others are feeling joy, too; and likewise when someone is in sorrow she shares a little of that with them as well.* Does she suffer from stigma and/or being ignored, abused? *I don't think so. We've had many little discussions about that and she tells me she doesn't suffer those things.*

5. What reasons did the health care workers give for asking that you put Michelle into an institution? *The doctors at the time assumed she would need too much care, too specialized types of care, too physically demanding care for a working-class mom and dad to be able to do while holding down jobs. They felt we'd burn out and possibly harm our own mental health further and give her substandard care.* What did you tell them in response? *I said we needed to at least give it a try, so that's what we did and are doing.* Is there stigma or public response? *We have not experienced stigma that I'm aware of. A few people are sometimes overly responsive to meeting her for the first time . . . talking to her too sweetly and thinking of her as a poor little waif or a lost puppy who needs a hug. But she seems ok with that . . . she just smiles patiently. Every so often a person or child will ask her what happened to her and she just says she got hurt a long time ago and needs to use her wheelchair to go places. But those people seem genuinely concerned for her as a person and her little answer is all they needed to feel comfortable around her.*

6. What do you think of people who put relatives into institutions, then just forget about their family member as though they were dead and buried. *I don't know if anyone would actually forget their family member. They may have to go on with their routine life out of necessity. There are probably many deep thoughts that they can't share but just aren't able to do any other thing. Everyone's life is different and so is how they must handle it.*

7. If you become tired, what gives you strength to go on? *Well, I'm a pretty lazy person, so I do not rely on my own strength to go on. As I mentioned, Michelle is a motivator. She's a pretty good manager and can judge when I need a little push. Also, we do things with friends and family or look for some cultural breath of fresh air. It's pretty much the same as anybody else in the world . . . you miss out on life if you don't go on.* Do you have a spiritual tradition that is helpful for you personally? *I was brought up in the Roman Catholic faith community, but have friends of all religions who've shared things they believe as well, so I guess I wouldn't say I rely on any one tradition in the strictest sense.*

Questions for Michelle:

1. How do you feel as a disabled person? *I just don't think about that very much. I just feel like me, just a person.* What do you find meaningful in life? *Doing things to help people how I can.* What is challenging for you personally? *I wish I could do some kinds of things a little better without any help.* What do you want to say to the world? *Nothing really. I don't feel like I need to say anything.*

2. How do you experience your religious faith? *I go to church and pray whenever I feel like it.* Do you find comfort and inspiration in your religious faith? *Yes.* Does it comfort you to go to St. Mary's? *I could go to any church, but I know more people at this one, so it's fun to see them there too. I guess that's comfort?*

3. What gives you strength to go on each day? *I don't exactly think it's any certain thing. I just do it.* What do you find interesting in life, and what do you enjoy doing? *People are interesting. I like seeing all the different things they do. I enjoy being around friends and my family. I enjoy being around animals. I enjoy reading and traveling.* What is fun for you and/or rewarding? *For fun I like to drive horses and ponies; going to a fair, ballgames, and things like that. I think it's rewarding to paint a picture that somebody likes or baking or cooking things and*

giving them to people to make them happy; being an aunt, helping children in the local elementary school learn to read.

◆ ◆ ◆

The place where I work: It is accessible and inclusive.

My former supervisor, a director of a patients' library in a local hospital, has created a space where people who have a physical, intellectual, emotional, or mental disability can find acceptance and inclusion while working side by side the able-bodied staff and volunteers. They serve the patients in the hospital. We find in this library volunteers who have developmental disorders, brain injuries, autism, as well as some types of mental illness. There are volunteers who must use wheel chairs and have little arm and/or hand mobility and others who use crutches. There are those who have difficulties speaking and forming words, and who may move slower physically. Yet, some of these last mentioned have minds as sharp as a tack and a quick wit. I've heard people call some of them retarded, which is not the case; it's quite the opposite. It must be hurtful for these disabled people when others treat them like they are intellectually deficient. It would take a lot of courage every day to face this kind of attitude.

Tom: Someone with a positive attitude.

One person who volunteers in this library is a man named Tom. He cannot use his legs; he has an electric wheelchair and has restricted use of his arms and hands. Tom said that when he was born he stopped breathing and it injured his brain and body. Now, middle-aged, he is a bit short and stout, balding. Tom laughs a lot and has a great sense of humor. He brings treats for all who work there to enjoy.

When I asked Tom about his disability, he answered: "There's always something gained. My experiences/condition made me what I am. If I didn't have this experience, I wouldn't be what I am today."

Now, that's a positive attitude!

Once Tom said that he doubted he could come to work the next day because his wheelchair had broken down and he needed to get it fixed. (There was a temporary fix so he could be there that day.) He said that he didn't want to stay home; that I should know that even though he wasn't there at the hospital volunteering, he really wanted to be there.[6]

Tom has a good attitude about serving others as a hospital volunteer and, I believe, has a very meaningful existence. I'm sure he feels appreciated at the hospital and welcome.

6. Personal interview, September 10, 2012

PART III

For Healing

THIS SECTION CONSISTS OF a presentation, essays, articles, and an interview that address many issues pertinent to the lives of those dealing with mental illness and/or physical, intellectual, emotional, or spiritual disability: loss of hope, loneliness, weakness, and rejection. Personal beliefs play a part in healing and recovery. Supportive networks and organizations can also foster healing and growth in an inclusive, supportive environment.

Presentation on Spirituality

Psychiatric Nursing Staff Education
University of Iowa Hospitals & Clinics
February 2009

[Excerpt from *Voices in the Rain: Meaning in Psychosis*]

Since I was only allowed on my bed at night I laid down on the couch in the dayroom and there withdrew into myself. With closed eyes I listened to the constant bombardment of voices. Disturbing memories of people and places consumed my thoughts. Passively, I gave in to despair, stopped thinking, and just let go. I had lost hope.

Even though people were all around me I ignored them. The staff urged me to sit up and socialize but I refused. Except for mealtimes, I stayed on the couch. Days passed.

Every evening before bed I lined up with the others at the nurses' station to receive medication with a small plastic cup of juice. I was also given vitamins after tests revealed malnutrition. Andrea, my nurse, told me that the medication was an antipsychotic to make the voices go away. But it had little effect. They persisted and I still had trouble sleeping.

One afternoon I felt an inner restlessness. Finding it hard to be still I stopped lying on the couch and starting pacing the hallways. When I found Andrea I complained to her.

"That could be akathisia," she said. "It's a side effect of the Stelazine you're taking. I'll talk to Dr. Taylor and we'll see what we can do."

That evening when I received my medication, I noticed two capsules in addition to the usual ones. I went to bed and within an hour fell asleep. About midnight I got up to go to the bathroom but halfway there I became faint and collapsed onto the floor. Through partially-opened eyes I vaguely saw two nurses bending over me, one holding my wrist while the other put a cuff around my arm.

"She's very pale," one said.

"It could be a reaction to the Mellaril," said the other.

I felt the cuff tighten.

"Her blood pressure is 58/40."

They discussed phoning the psychiatrist and helped me up. A nurse took my arm, assisting me to the bathroom *and then back to my room. I slept fitfully through the rest of the night.*

I did not receive medication the next day. The following evening I noticed pills of a color different from the ones I had been given before. With this change I experienced a day to day decrease in the volume and frequency of voices. After two weeks they disappeared except for faint noises at bedtime and I started to sleep on a more consistent basis at night.

My reaction to the stillness was muted by the shock of what I had endured for almost two years. The onslaught from another realm had left me devasted. My newly found sanity was frail and my emotions, unsteady.

After I was discharged from the hospital, I continued to take the medication and eventually became more involved with various programs aimed at furthering my independence. These practical steps toward improving my situation were acts of faith on my part and I wanted to comply. After all, these people were the experts and knew what was best. They were doing all they could. Yet I wanted more. I wanted to know what had happened to me. I wanted to know the meaning of my suffering, the reason why I had gotten ill. All the external props would have little effect unless my innermost being could find the answers. Until then my soul would not be satisfied and my mind would not be healed.

I'm going to talk about how spirituality, alongside of biology and other factors, is an integral part of recovery and is essential for healing the emotional and psychological suffering inherent in illness.

Out of spirituality comes hope. Having hope allows for the possibility of change. When a person is unable to envision possibilities of change, they see no future. And without a future there is only despair. According to Danish philosopher, Soren Kierkegaard, in his book, *The Sickness Unto Death*, it is impossible to understand despair without understanding spirit.[1] Despair, or lack of hope, is a spiritual disease with biological components often leading to death.

---

1. Kierkegaard, *Sickness Unto Death*, 34.

Therefore, one of the primary goals of a health care provider would be to first instill hope, and from there all things are possible: healing is possible, recovery is possible. With hope, there is a possibility of change and a future. Kierkegaard wrote that *possibility is for the self what oxygen is for breathing.*[2]

Brenda Shostrum, PhD, formerly a psychiatric nurse and past Professor and Chair of the Nursing Department at Coe College, has taught on the subject of spirituality and health. In regard to this she says that the medical field has so focused on biological cure in the past one hundred years that during this time it has neglected to heal the suffering which is involved when a person is ill.[3] Disease can be a traumatic event and, conversely, emotional and spiritual trauma has an impact upon human biology. Therefore, events can cause biological disease.[4]

The term *disease* can be thought of differently than the term *sickness.* With sickness, healing is spiritual. *The medical field has so focused on cure that it is forgetting that healing is spiritual.*[5] Emotional pain of illness including psychological losses, mental confusion, and grief, all contribute to despair which effect biology. Therefore, I believe that a holistic health care provider will not neglect one aspect of existence in favor of another, but is one who seeks to maintain a balanced view of the different dimensions of the human phenomenon.

What is meant by the term, *spirituality*, and how does it relate to the word, *religion*?

Spirituality is that which animates or gives life to physical organisms.[6]

Author Timothy Keller says that in a general sense, religion may be simply a worldview or set of faith-based assumptions about the nature of things whether in a materialistic context or spiritual one. Everyone has such assumptions about reality and this is how

---

2. Kierkegaard, *Sickness Unto Death*, 62.
3. Shostrum, *Spirituality and Health*, Presentation.
4. Shostrum, *Spirituality and Health*, Presentation.
5. Shostrum, *Spirituality and Health*, Presentation.
6. Merriam-Webster, https://www.merriam-webster.com/dictionary/spirit

we operate in our daily lives. For some people their worldview is thought out and reflected upon and, for others, it is not. Everyone has their own views about what people are for, about the purpose of human life, and ideas about how we should live. These beliefs or assumptions are what we base our lives on and are the reasons we go to work, form relationships, and set goals.[7]

A spiritual perspective may be a natural extension of our worldview that often involves faith in a Higher Power. There is strong research evidence which indicates that faith is associated with positive health outcomes. As health care providers on psychiatric units you've witnessed countless examples of despairing patients whose lives reflect devastation, pain, and loss. So I would like to ask you: What happens when a person with mental illness loses hope?

According to an article published in 2008 in the American Journal of Preventative Medicine, "in 2005, based on the most recent data available, the rate of suicide in the US was 11 per 100,000. In 2005 suicide claimed 32,637 lives and was the fourth leading cause of death for people aged ten to fourteen years."[8] The article stated that one of the risk factors for suicide is hopelessness.[9] And as you probably already know, the absence of social supports has been repeatedly shown to be associated with elevated mortality. Participation in a religious community not only enhances the ability to cope with stress, it also fosters social integration which is then a protection against suicide.

I, personally, have found valuable support in this way. I've gained a sense of belonging, and when I've gone through periods of depression in recent years they do not last as long as in the past. Since I've made new friends I have found better ways to cope with life's problems.

---

7. Keller, *Reason for God*, 15.
8. Hu et al., "Mid-Life Suicide," 589.
9. Hu et al., "Mid-Life Suicide," 589.

So once again: spirituality can inspire hope. With hope, there is a possibility of change and a future. *Possibility is for the self what oxygen is for breathing.*[10]

One researcher, a psychiatrist, Dr. Harold G. Koenig, has written extensively on the role of faith in healing the body, mind, and spirit—which are all interrelated. One authoritative work he co-authored is, *The Handbook of Religion and Health*.[11] In my reading of these materials I have found studies that support the assertion that faith increases self-control or self- efficacy in people with mental illness,[12] as well as, enabling them to cope and recover. Another term for this is an *internal locus of control*.[13] It has been my experience that my spiritual life has increased my self-efficacy as seen in the internal locus of control. I have been able to set goals and achieve them, some of which have to do with meaningful work and others with physical health.

I know that sometimes you may encounter patients who have pathological delusions of a religious nature. As health care providers it would be important to be able to differentiate between the helpful, positive aspects of spiritual beliefs and those that are detrimental.

As I look back over my life, I can see that devastation often spoke to me in ways that happiness has not. After many years of struggles my life reached the lowest depth of despair the night I nearly succeeded in killing myself at the age of thirty-nine. This experience made it clear that my way of life was not working. I needed help. I then used determination and the freedom of choice to return to a life of faith and was empowered in ways I never thought possible. I was enabled to build a new life that uses my gifts and abilities and allows me to contribute to society.

As a writer I hope to improve treatments for people who have a mental illness and reduce stigma. The excerpt I opened my talk with is from my book-length memoir, *Voices in the Rain*, which is

---

10. Kierkegaard, *Sickness Unto Death*, 62.
11. Koenig et al., *Handbook of Religion and Health*.
12. Koenig et al., *Handbook of Religion and Health*, 211.
13. Koenig et al., *Handbook of Religion and Health*, 210.

about my life and experience with mental illness and my entry into the recovery process.[14] You can also find some of my other writing at my website: https://www.hopeforrecovery.com/.

In closing, I'd like to say that as health care providers there is much you can do to lessen the suffering caused by the trauma of mental illness, all of which is interrelated with biology and biological disease. First, continued research is needed to provide more effective medications. And second, I believe it would be helpful if treatment options remain favorable to supporting what really matters to patients. Often, among other things, it is their spirituality, something that can have a powerful impact upon their lives. It is something that may bring about emotional and psychological improvements and may inspire hope. For as I said before, *with hope, there is a possibility of change and a future.*

In my experience of being a patient I have found it helpful when my health care providers did not neglect one aspect of existence in favor of another, but who, instead, sought to maintain a balanced view of the different dimensions of the human phenomenon.

Thank you for allowing me to be here and, thank you, for all you are doing to help those who suffer with the affliction of a mental disorder.

---

14. Murphy, *Voices in the Rain.*

More God, Less Psychiatric Illness

Devotions for Those in Recovery from Mental Illness

Marcia A. Murphy, contributing editor
with Myrna Farraj, co-editor.

Cedar Rapids: Eagle Book Bindery (2017)
Book Extracts

GOD CARES: GOD IS CLOSE TO THE BROKENHEARTED

Life is full of suffering. That is a truth no one can deny, whatever one's background. As a Christian I've learned that I can find meaning in suffering and in carrying my cross. But sometimes the sadness in my heart is so overpowering that my faith is challenged. I may question whether God really does love me. I may feel abandoned by family, friends, neighbors, and coworkers—utterly alone in the world. People with good intentions will recite verses to me about being still and knowing that God is there. Yet, they are often the ones with people around them, with spouses and children and grandchildren who comfort them. But it is likely that they, too, have experienced isolation during some point of their lives.

During the times I have felt lonely I have turned to history, to those who've gone before. I am led by an inner voice or compass that directs and guides me. These historical people are my friends and as I study their lives, mentors appear in my mind touching my heart: feed the poor; liberate the oppressed; stand up for justice. I find this comforting God through books, films, photos, and I follow where God is leading me. My life unfolds by the inner workings of the Holy Spirit motivating and inspiring me to go forward—building on the foundations of those brave souls of the past who often spoke of a deep loneliness, but still doing what they could to further God's Kingdom.[1]

GOD LOVES THE OUTCASTS

Someone said that people with a mental illness are the lepers of modern-day society. If this is true one may have felt rejected by those who appear socially successful. They have all the right college degrees, beautiful houses, fashionable clothes, and say all the right things. On the surface it looks like God has blessed them exclusively with abundance, wealth, health, and an easy life. But looking below the surface we may see signs of a deceptive self-sufficiency,

---

1. Murphy, "God Cares," 1.

self-perceived independence, and overconfidence—things that stand in the way of acknowledging God as their maker and sustainer, the one whom they need to depend on. To suffer from mental illness in all of its emotional trauma and very real challenges of not only physical deprivations, but also social exclusion, can often bring one to one's knees. It is there that we find that Jesus Christ is all we have. It is our God who provides us with all that we need to live. It is God that sustains us. By joining with a religious community, we can find acceptance in a concrete visible form of brothers and sisters in Christ who offer a helping hand. And like the leper that Christ reached out to and touched with compassion, we will be healed, finding a new life full of meaning and purpose. Under God's wings we will find shelter.[2]

OUR ANGER: WHAT WE DO WITH OUR OWN RAGE

I don't know about you, but over the years I've had trouble with anger—and what to do with it. People have treated me badly, some because they don't like those with a mental illness. They may think we are all dumb, uneducated, lazy, good for nothings. Our medications may cause weight gain so people think we overeat and lack self-discipline. When I've been abused I've asked God: "Why this curse?! Why do you hate me?! Did you give me my mental illness?! What have I done to deserve this punishment?! Answer me!!" Then I remember the story of the blind man in the Bible, who was born blind and Jesus said: "It is not because he sinned or his parents sinned that he was born blind. But he is blind so that the work of God might be displayed in his life." These words can soothe my soul and I can understand that all things work together for good if we love God. God can take the most painful, awful things and turn them into a positive force for the good. In the end, justice will prevail because God loves us.[3]

---

2. Murphy, "God Loves the Outcasts," 2–3.
3. Murphy, "Our Anger," 5.

More God, Less Psychiatric Illness

HOW DO WE BECOME INSPIRED?

When I feel loved, I am inspired. I can climb mountains and scale a wall (metaphorically speaking). However, love in the imagination is a dream while love in reality can be difficult: *Love in action is a harsh and dreadful thing compared to love in dreams.*[4]

I've heard that giving new life by physically giving birth to a child is no picnic. A parent working most days, all day long, to put food on the table for the family requires great emotional and physical sacrifice. When we look at our Lord God we see someone who cares for the poor, the outcasts, lame, and handicapped—those whom our society deems unworthy of respect. We see around us the love of doctors caring for their patients; pastors watching over their flocks, and teachers guiding their students. Though friends may desert us, there is someone who sticks closer than a brother. He died on a cross, suffering the humiliation of nakedness, with nails through his hands and feet. He experienced death so you and I would not have to. He took on God's wrath for the sinfulness of all humanity, suffering separation from God the Father so you and I could be united with God both here on earth and in Heaven through all eternity. Now, that's real love. No doubt about it.[5]

LIFE CHOICES: WHAT DO WE LIVE FOR?

The alternative of living for God is focusing on ourselves. If we love ourselves more than anything else, there is no room left to love others. People live in relation to others while on earth. It is impossible to avoid people. How we choose to live determines the quality of our spiritual life. To ignore the spiritual side is to live in a materialistic mindset. Then we seek fulfillment in fancy cars, but they do not satisfy; in sexual promiscuity, but find it destructive; in food and drink, but we never are satiated; in entertainment and self-gratification, but we end up feeling empty. If we as Christians believe that God is our sustainer and provider, then only through our

---

4. Dostoyevsky, *Brothers Karamazov*, 58.
5. Murphy, "How Do We Become Inspired?" 13.

connection to him will we find all that we need: then relationships fall into place; our work is fulfilling; we find meaning in suffering and strength to endure. Without God, we sink into the depths of despair and find no way out. But with the light of Christ, we find the path of peace, comfort and hope for the future.[6]

WHAT DOES IT MEAN TO LOVE GOD?

We love God when we obey God. Emotions come and go. They are fleeting. How we conduct our lives says more. God gives his commands in the Bible, his word. In Exodus 20:1–17 we find the Ten Commandments. The New Testament lessons teach us how to obey. Through the parables and words of Christ and his followers, clear directions are given. They center around loving God and our neighbor. Who is our neighbor? All the people around us; no more, no less.[7]

OUR ACTIONS SPEAK LOUDER THAN WORDS

We live by what our values dictate. Our values are displayed to the world by what we do. We choose our values by what we love. How we spend our time says what we love and therefore, value. We also become what we value because we worship what we value and become what we worship. We were created to worship God, the Holy Trinity: God the Father, Son, and Holy Spirit. We can learn what God is like and who he is by reading the Bible and seeing who Jesus Christ was in the New Testament. Asking God in prayer, *who are you?* and *how can I know and understand my relationship with you?* is the beginning to knowing God and becoming like him.[8]

---

6. Murphy, "Life Choices," 16.
7. Murphy, "What Does It Mean to Love God?" 17.
8. Murphy, "Our Actions," 18.

GOOD GOES IN—GOOD COMES OUT

We live by what is in our heads, or you could say—our minds. If we fill our minds with junk: violence, profanity, judgments, hatred, jealousy, greed, immorality, or deceit, then these things are creating our personalities which is what the world will see in us. However, if we fill our minds with loving, healthy, and pure thoughts like peace, loyalty, compassion, generosity, kindness, altruism, virtue, honesty, then this will become our personalities—what the world sees when it looks at us. The more we fill our minds with God's holy Word, the more we will be transformed to reflect God's nature.[9]

---

9. Murphy, "Good Goes In," 18–19.

Access & Inclusive Mission Handbook

*An Interview with the
Reverend Timothy H. Little, DMin, BCC*

CONDUCTED AND WRITTEN BY MARCIA A. MURPHY,
MODERATOR, PEIA AIM NETWORK

Interview Skyped/Taped on February 5 & 19, 2016

This interview was conducted by Marcia A. Murphy with the Reverend Dr. Timothy H. Little, DMin (Doctor of Ministry), BCC (Board Certified Chaplain), ACPE Supervisor (Association of Clinical Pastoral Education), Retired Chaplain, Pastoral/Spiritual Counselor/Therapist. Reverend Little was born without sight in his right eye and only limited vision of 20/200 in his left eye. He lived his entire life with this visual impairment until the mid-1990s when he also lost sight in his left eye, making him totally blind. He is the founder of AIM (Access and Inclusive Mission) in Sacramento, California.

The focus of AIM is to increase disability awareness and inclusion for those with physical, intellectual, emotional, and spiritual challenges, encouraging our religious and civic communities to be welcoming places for all. As an advocate for disabled persons, Marcia A. Murphy of St. Andrew Presbyterian Church of Iowa City, IA, applied for, and gained approval from the Presbytery of East Iowa (PEIA) leadership to officially establish the PEIA AIM Presbytery Network in 2014.

Marcia: *Rev. Little, could you please tell us a little about yourself? What is your background, your career, and things that brought you to the point of starting an AIM committee at your church? What was it in your life that brought you to that?*

Rev. Little: I will start with my background and what got me concerned for AIM work: My background starts with the fact that I was born too soon. I was very premature and therefore was a very tiny tot. While given a much more obnoxious name (Archibald Alexander Little, III) which was carrying on family traditions, I ended up mostly being called, Tiny Tim. And it wasn't until I was about eleven or twelve years old that I had a chance to pick my own name. That's when I picked Timothy. But in some sense being small, being tiny, having a struggle with health in early life, was a big factor. I was the child of two physicians, two pediatricians, and obviously they and their community took very good care of me.

I did at birth and for most of my life have 20/200 vision in my left eye and nothing in my right eye. And I think that in many ways that, basically, set some things in motion: the fact that my parents were doctors, the fact that I didn't see well, and the fact that I was well cared for and, moreover, that I was in a family that valued education. I was really very much supported in my education and at one point, in the fourth grade, I was sent away to Perkins Institute School for the Blind in Watertown, near Boston, Massachusetts, to learn how to use Braille. I don't know how to use Braille today, but I did for quite a while then. And I learned something, I think, by being at Perkins about how much effort went into helping persons with sight difficulty to actually cope with the world in which we live in spite of the disability.

I'm sure that had a lot to do with the rest of the decisions I made growing up partly because I never saw myself as second class but I did understand myself as a person with a disability and that I needed to do those things which help to overcome that disability so that I could live as much a normal and marvelous life as possible. And I think that also had a lot to do with my attitude, as well as issues that I studied over time and the sense of my call into the ministry as opposed to—I might have been called to science if I followed my parent's group. My disability influenced the direction of my call into ministry and my sense of being able to participate in helping others with physical and subsequently, emotional disabilities.

I was much more aware, growing up, of persons with physical disabilities as opposed to persons with emotional or learning disabilities. I think that background had a lot to do with setting me on a path that included more than forty years as a chaplain and, probably, as a person with concerns for helping religious communities reach out and be inclusive of those with disabilities. That's a long answer to your question, I think.

Marcia: *Rev. Little, please continue with your story.*

Rev. Little: I did much of my training at Andover Newton Theological Seminary and then with the CPE program at Boston State Hospital and Boston City Hospital. I knew that I wanted to be a chaplain in a mental health setting and I looked around the country and sent out my qualifications. I eventually chose, after several visits, to accept a call to the Mental Health Institute in Iowa. Now I spent only about three years there in Iowa. My wife and I lived in Mt. Pleasant, a very small town and we were very much a part of the local church there and were concerned about social justice issues and my wife, Sandy, was an observer on the school board, and so forth. But then we received a call to the Georgia Mental Health Institute where I was for eighteen years. Then in 1988, we came out to Sacramento, to the University of California Davis Medical Center to essentially start a clinical pastoral education program (chaplaincy program), there for UCD Medical Center. It was when we were here in Sacramento that after a while we became members of Westminster Presbyterian Church, one of the major downtown Presbyterian churches.

Very early on—I probably need to say—my wife, as an adolescent, got polio, and throughout her life exceeded what her body could allow her to do, and by the time we came out here to Sacramento she was using a power-chair. And that probably had something to do with our developing the AIM committee at Westminster Presbyterian Church.

The parking lot at Westminster was in the back of the church. The backdoor, which was the best way into the church, had four steps so her chair was not going to go in the back. We had to go around to the front and actually go past the front door to a side door that had a ramp up into a courtyard to allow her to go into the church. The committee very quickly talked and said, "Could we do something about putting a ramp down the back stairs?" They were not steep stairs; they were really very sloping stairs. But at first we spent a lot of time in deciding we couldn't do a ramp, it was going to cost a lot of money.

Finally, the AIM committee took a look at it and together with the pastor we put some boards down that allowed those steps to be traveled as a ramp. It was a little shaky but we found out we could in fact build a ramp. It was not going to be quite satisfactory for the standards that are dictated by the rules regarding ramps but it was going to be pretty close. And it was very easy. Sometime later our AIM committee saw that we needed to do something about an opener on the door from the ramp in front that opened into the sanctuary. And one of our people on the committee decided to make that a memorial contribution to honor her mother.

What I'm saying is, all sorts of projects began to develop including deciding to make some pew openings—shortening some pews—so that people in chairs could be close to family as opposed to having to sit up front or out back.

So the committee got formed to do some very practical kinds of things and began to discover more and more how to rearrange the bathrooms so they could be more accessible for people with wheelchairs. The committee began while looking for very practical answers to help the church find ways—without spending an arm and a leg—to change some things. And, finally, our elevator broke down and that took a good bit of money to fix, to make it work right. One of the things that that included was putting a phone inside the elevator so that if someone got stuck they could still phone out.

Marcia: *Were there any attitudinal barriers to work on?*

Rev. Little: It may be that the physical barriers are the easiest to address. I think the attitudinal issues are a little more difficult. I think there is a natural tendency on our part to respond in a certain way to persons who are different than ourselves, whether it's racial or ethnic, and certainly people with obvious disabilities, physical or emotional. There is a resistance, an unconscious tendency to not be quite comfortable with persons with disabilities and we need to work on overcoming that. How do we do that? By exposing ourselves to a lot of persons with disabilities, by welcoming folks, by going up to them and introducing ourselves—welcoming them as we would welcome anyone and to begin to ask them how can we best meet their needs? How can we best serve them? How can we best incorporate them into our life together as people trying to care for one another? And sometimes that's going to get us into some very difficult situations, but we need to stay with it and overcome some of our resistance and our unconscious tendency to pull away.

While I've talked about some very practical changes that the AIM committee sought to make for our congregation, i.e., to make it more accessible, the real issue is that people with disabling conditions often are experienced by members of the congregation, who don't share disabilities, as being different. And being different, we then tend to not be as welcoming to them. Now, nobody in the church is intentionally rejecting any person. But we all have a tendency to feel some degree of difficulty in reaching out to people who are very different from ourselves. And the more different they are, the more difficult it is for us to bridge the barrier. And often, our hesitation and uneasiness are hardly even known to us—we have to reflect very much to be able to break through our own resistance. I think that is especially true with people who have learning disabilities or who have weird ways of dealing with speech, those with difficulties dealing with emotions. And a lot of times we don't intend to be rejecting but we're not necessarily welcoming.

If you would look at the biblical story of the blind man to whom Jesus was able to restore sight, a lot of people were upset that Jesus restored his sight because a disability was by definition caused because someone had sinned. So we dealt with our unconscious uncomfortableness by assuming they sinned or his or her parents must have sinned.

The other issue was that the young man whose sight was restored disrupted the social welfare system of his day in as much as he had been sitting on the side of the road with a bowl or something to receive handouts, and people could feel good because they were helping him out not seeing that they were making him dependent upon their meager contributions. Since the disabled weren't receiving their dues anymore, they weren't feeling so good anymore. And I think that has a lot to say about how we reach out to persons with disabilities in our churches. I can't think of a church that would say up front, "We don't want any people with disabilities in our church." Every church I've known about wants to draw people in, that's the intention. But many churches don't quite know how, how to overcome their own uncomfortableness with people with disabilities; and how to respect persons with disabilities as children of God with a disability.

My disability does not define entirely who I am. It does give me a challenge. It means I have to think about things in a different way; but it does not define who I am. I'm not, therefore, the blind man. I happen to be blind and this is part of who I am as a person and to be celebrated, and not to be a barrier between us. Now one of the things that means—and sometimes I have to tell people this—if people come up and start talking to me, it is helpful if they tell me who they are, even if they have a name tag on, this doesn't do me a bit of good! And while I get fairly comfortable with learning people's voice tone, I don't always know how to recognize someone. Most people can look around them to see who people are because they can see physical conditions; but, even so, we all need to greet one another by name to remind one another who we are as opposed to assuming we can figure that out. That's a welcoming gesture for people, at least those who want to come to engage me in conversation.

The other thing that happens—and this happens a lot at church—at times after the worship service there will be a big crowd and we're milling around at fellowship hour and sharing together, and I'll be talking to somebody and all of a sudden they're not there but I don't know that. They've caught the eye of somebody across the room and are headed across the room, and it does feel a little silly for me to be talking to thin air. So I think persons in our congregations need to think carefully about how we welcome one another into the fellowship of the church and it is very important that churches be places that support and encourage one another not only in the faith, but in all walks of life.

Marcia: *Rev. Little, if you were to create a mission statement for AIM work, how would you summarize it within a few sentences?*

Rev. Little: I would include in the mission statement for an AIM Committee the following objectives:

1. Become actively involved in welcoming persons with disabling conditions into the congregation.
2. Evaluate the physical building plan for ways in which the church can be more welcoming.
3. Assist leaders, committees, and the congregation to reflect on ways in which they have resisted reaching out to persons with disabling conditions and to help them learn how to put forward a more positive welcoming atmosphere.

Marcia: *Rev. Little, what are some ways for an AIM committee or church to accomplish the AIM objectives or goals?*

Rev. Little: I think for us to deal with our own internal resistance, attitudes, our biases, we need to find opportunities to reach out and welcome persons with disabilities into our fellowship, to look for opportunities to gather together. It may well be that we need to go out of the church to where people are, where people are gathering with particular disabilities. A case in point: We at Westminster thought that we needed to welcome people who are hard of hearing into our fellowship. One of the things we did was that a couple of members of our AIM committee went and met with the Association of Hearing Disabled Persons. And what we discovered was that they have a hard time meeting with us, meeting with hearing and sighted congregations and they have a need for a special kind of equipment and hand signing. They gather together to support one another and they were really not prepared to come and join us. We did not continue with the project. I think we could have continued by saying to them that our building or location is open to you to use and then maybe over time you will feel comfortable in actually engaging with us in a way that can be useful for you and to us. We didn't go that far, but I think it might have been the next practical step; plus, to say our fellowship hall is yours for no cost at all.

Marcia: *Rev. Little, how did you find people to be members of your AIM committee at Westminster?*

Rev. Little: First of all, a couple of people I talked with said, "I think it's a good idea." A person I was comfortable with said, "I'll chair it!" And I said, "Great; that's absolutely wonderful!" And she was an elder so she sort of had priority in that sense. We just gathered a few people around us. After we had been meeting for about three years, a young lady and her husband joined the church and she was poorly sighted, blind, and she was on a state board for offering services for the blind. So, of course, we captured those people into our work. We kept looking for people we could talk into being part of the team. We did not have to worry about issues of whether they could be voted on or not. We essentially formed a committee that was willing to work together around these issues.

Marcia: *Thank you. Now to a broader stance, how would you relate the topic of social justice with disability awareness and inclusion in the churches and in the greater community? What are your thoughts on that?*

Rev. Little: Okay, I think the first thing that I would want to look at is that there has been legislation since the 1960s that tries to acknowledge that there are things as a society or a country that we need to provide more effectively for persons with disabling conditions. There was some good effort but an awful lot of people didn't benefit for a long time. Employment for persons who are blind still isn't very good. Now I have to say I've been fortunate in that I've been fairly well open to employment. But there are a lot of blind people, people with a disability, and that disability gets in the way of their being able to be employed. There's a whole issue of, for instance, stores being more welcoming by fixing the problem of steps, being open to allowing people to come in whether they have wheelchairs or they walk well, and so forth.

I remember early on in our time in Sacramento, someone took us to a restaurant and we discovered that the restaurant really was up on the second floor and that the only way for my wife, in her chair, to enter the restaurant, was to be taken up on an elevator which was used by the restaurant to bring up food and to bring all the garbage back down. So it was not a very convenient way to get us into that restaurant.

Now some of the laws regarding open accommodation have been strengthened over the years, certainly in the nineties and the first part of 2000. There have been improvements some of which have resulted in providing better for our military folks returning with major disabilities. But we certainly need to be a more open country in terms of what needs to take place. It is still very easy to go to a hotel and ask for the accommodations for disability and to discover that what is being provided just isn't adequate. The important thing is we've come a long way, and the church has not always been out front in this. It has taken churches a long time to realize what barriers there are to full participation for persons with disabilities.

In some sense churches are in a unique situation. They cannot be sued like stores can be sued or restaurants can be sued for not providing adequate accommodations. For instance, a restaurant can be sued if they refuse to allow a guide dog. A friend of mine who is totally blind had to take a restaurant to court for not letting his seeing-eye dog accompany him into the restaurant. A church as a non-profit corporation, can't be sued for having too many steps, not having accommodations for restrooms, an elevator, or the like, because it is a non-profit corporation. However, if they are open three to four nights for a theatrical production or operate a preschool and they are making money off that, they can be sued for not providing adequate accommodations. It shouldn't take a lot of effort for churches to realize that churches really ought to be leaders, not followers, in setting the standards for persons with disabilities.

Marcia: *Rev. Little, please reflect upon your own personal experience now and could you tell me, did you find a special meaning or purpose for your life as a direct result from your having a disability condition; and, if so, how did that shape your particular perspective on life?*

Rev. Little: I think very early I accepted my disability as something natural and something I simply needed to live with, and that it wasn't good or bad, it simply was. I know that over time, I have come to appreciate it as a particular gift. Yes, there are challenges that it presents me with; but probably more importantly, there are gifts which it grants to me. A minor one, but it's still important: my wife and I raised three children but I was never called upon to be the chauffer because of my disability. My wife had to get the children from place to place. Sometimes I felt somewhat guilty that I couldn't help her. Yet, in reality, I felt relieved from not having that responsibility.

I think also, I was born with the gift of optimism and I had good support, and my sight impairment was a not a particular deterrent. My disability was something I could live with and enjoy and I could overcome its disability features, but at the same time discover its advantages.

Marcia: *I recently saw the results of a study[1] that concluded that the majority of disabled persons do not attend religious services or take part in a religious community. My ideas about that are that a lot of disabled people are of lower income and do not own a vehicle, making it difficult or almost impossible to get to a church. So this is a big economic barrier. What are your thoughts on that?*

---

1. https://drgrcevich.wordpress.com/

Rev. Little: I think that a lot of people with disabilities do have a resistance to reaching out. I think a lot of us are somewhat cautious concerning whether differentness will or will not be accepted. But I do think that sometimes the barrier is that we are not ready to welcome. So then we really have to look at that. We have to acknowledge that there are people with serious disabilities who do not expect to be welcome and therefore in some sense determine that they will not be welcomed by never showing up. I think the way to overcome this is for church folks to seriously reach out to persons with disabilities and encourage them to come and be a part of the church. It takes a lot of encouragement. I think in the first place we need to be sensitive to those parents who are struggling to raise their children who have a disability. The church needs to go the second mile to reach out so that they and their children will feel welcomed into our fellowship. I think every parent of a disabled child needs the community to come forward and incorporate them into their life.

I think as we discover that there are people with certain disabilities that gather together, that this offers us opportunities. I know that at one point there was a serious outreach to invite to a luncheon on a regular basis, people who are mentally ill. And somehow the contact was made with those persons maybe through the hospital, maybe through the community agencies serving persons with mental illness. We first invited them to lunch and then after time, into a more permanent way of joining in with the church fellowship. Sometimes you need to take the church to these people instead of supposing they will come to church.

People with a mental illness have a hard barrier to overcome. They have been rejected so often that it is very difficult for these people to reach out or to *respond* to your invitation. It takes work, again, again, and again. It is a matter of building that sense of trust, that sense of confidence that they can begin to trust you in a way that they haven't been able to trust very many people. And I don't know if there's any easy answer—it's just hard. That is why it's not as difficult reaching out to parents who have children with a disability of one kind or another, it is probably easier because some of those parents know they need help, know they need support. Once we've built this wall around ourselves in terms of being able to respond to the invitation, it's hard to break down these walls and to try. Particularly since many of the people with emotional disabilities have tried to break through the walls any number of times as they were growing up and have found that the wall doesn't give very easily and that people are more apt to just disregard them or mock them, make fun of them, or to take advantage of them.

You also mentioned, and I think this is another issue, that sometimes people with disabilities are essentially people without income. Some of that is in our fault as a culture. We don't make it very easy for people with disabling conditions to earn a decent wage. I was very lucky. I never got rich, but there are a lot of people who are blind who don't ever get offered a job who have difficulty finding employment. There are people who are disabled because they have low IQ or they have difficulty getting around. Physical disabilities probably get in the way least often. But even there, they may walk into a business and apply and the business says, "We don't need a person who can't move fast in our business." There is prejudice against employment of persons with disabilities—it's against the law to screen them out—but nevertheless, in a large number of situations, people with disabling conditions simply don't get employment or don't get adequate employment. They get very poor wages; they might get welcomed into a job that might pay nine dollars an hour. That is not a living wage.

Marcia: Rev. Little, how can the church be a spotlight or leader for the wider culture? What can the AIM committee do to help change societal attitudes? How can the AIM committee energize religious communities to deal with all these different issues?

Rev. Little: I think in the first place members of the AIM committee, and maybe drawing upon others in the congregation, need to do a very serious survey, looking at the community that you're serving. What are the issues? What does the community do? Does it have a survey of who is homeless? What is it doing to address the issue of homeless? What are the issues that maintain people being homeless? Is it racial? Is it ethnic? Is it mental health? Is it substance abuse? Is it a whole number of different things? Nobody wishes to be homeless. You cannot convince me that anyone wishes to be homeless. There are people who have tried and tried and tried. And then rather than being crammed into a center and have to get up to get out of it at seven o'clock in the morning, may choose to camp along the river. For instance here in Sacramento, we have people who are camping out. That's technically against the law. Most of our communities make people who are homeless, criminals. We need to change that around. And the church needs to be about this business. The church needs to call this situation to the attention of the community and then say as a community that we need to find ways to provide housing.

As a community we need to provide ways for people who are homeless to be able to sit in the park, have a place to go to the bathroom, have a place to hang out, and have a place where they can be welcomed into our community. We need to work at that and overcome our tendency to be fearful of persons who are disabled, fearful of persons who are homeless because of disability or another thing. We all need to see that as an issue and that we need to do something very different than what we normally do; and that is to make sure that we see the responsibility to tax in a certain way. If every home in the county has a tax levied on it that is designated to provide housing for the homeless, we would see some differences.

Marcia: *Rev. Little, I've come to the end of my list of questions. Is there anything else you'd like to add or emphasize for your closing words?*

Rev. Little: I do think that working to break down the barriers for inclusion in our congregations, but also the issue to some extent to break down the barriers for full participation in the life of your community, all is part of a very challenging issue because we are comfortable being with people like ourselves. We all live with some degree of bias and we need to recognize that we all are more comfortable being with people like ourselves. And, therefore, to reach out beyond that, to reach out to welcome people who are different than ourselves, to seek opportunities to reach out, is not an easy task. We need to recognize that it takes a lot of courage, it takes a lot of steadfast willingness to do it over and over and over again, as we open our doors, open our hearts, open our minds, and welcome people into life together with us.

Farewell

Previously published in
You are entering your life: An Anthology of the PatientVoice Project
Edited by Austin Bunn and April Kopp (2008) 30–36.

A select few of the University of Iowa Writers' Workshop participants tutored and directed several individuals from within the larger community who at some point in their lives, experienced some kind of disability: mental, physical, or otherwise. The fruit of the classes and instruction became a book, an anthology, consisting of short pieces giving voice to what it feels like to be a patient in recovery; or in some cases, without. The prompt below gave the direction for this piece of creative non-fiction. Except for my own, the names mentioned in the work are pseudonyms.

Prompt: Write about something that happened that was important to you, an experience or memory that evokes strong feelings. Instructor: Tim O'Sullivan

The Collected Writings of Marcia A. Murphy

I sat in the psychiatric clinic waiting for Dr. Hayes. This would be my last appointment with him. A few other patients waited for their therapists. A man and a woman engaged in a loud conversation about anti-depressants: Prozac had helped her lose weight, she said triumphantly; Trazadone had made him gain. A magazine rack near the back of the room offered diversion with its wrinkled and torn magazines: *Good Housekeeping, Ladies' Home Journal, Newsweek,* and *People*. But I had no desire to read. I just looked at the pastoral scenes of trees and grassy hills hanging on the wall in front of me.

After this appointment my life would drastically change and I wasn't sure if it would be for the better. I wondered how I would survive. Who would be my new psychiatrist? Maybe Dr. Hayes would have something to say about that.

I had on my church clothes, a dark gray pair of slacks with a dress jacket and black low-heeled dress shoes. My brown hair was pulled back in a low-riding ponytail: my usual no-nonsense style.

He appeared near the receptionist's desk. He was thin and had been ever since I'd met him. And tall, probably six foot two or so. His shoulders were slightly bent over, rounded a bit from decades of study, writing, and from the burden of heavy workloads and grave responsibilities: not only from taking care of hundreds of patients, but from teaching in the medical school, doing research, and publishing.

After Dr. Hayes nodded at me I got up, put my backpack over my shoulder, and walked over to grasp his outstretched hand. His handshake was firm, yet gentle. It was the same hand that twenty-five years before had reached down to a psychologically bruised and broken mental patient.

When Dr. Hayes first saw me as a patient, I was severely ill. I had just spent three and a half years in the Unification Church, a cult. The whirlwind schedule of fundraising and attempts at recruiting others proved to be a constant source or humiliation. Misdirected spiritual practices as well as sleep and nutritional deprivation wreaked havoc on my mind. On top of this, cult leaders maintained an aggressive attack with constant brainwashing lectures on church doctrine. Already mentally unstable before I joined the cult, my involvement in this group magnified my problems, and

I started to hear terrifying hallucinations. I fought for the survival of my psychological life.

The trauma of those cult years extended into post-cult life. After being hospitalized and discharged, the ability to find or maintain a religious faith continued to be a challenge. At that point I had to decide if I would accept God's help which came through Dr. Hayes and the psychiatric establishment.

As a psychiatrist, according to the traditional definition, Dr. Hayes was a healer of the soul. As such, he had asked once at the beginning of treatment, "Do you believe in God?"

To which I answered, "I want to, but I can't."

Doctor Hayes and I walked down the hall to his office. As usual, he walked beside me. Some psychiatrists go ahead of the patient, which is not wrong; yet Dr. Hayes was always at my side, physically and metaphorically, as a means of support. I had not always appreciated this stoic friend; in fact, once I had even run away. Having misunderstood something he said, in a childish tantrum, I vowed to never return. I stayed away for two years. But when I came back I found him still willing to support me in desperate times—times of confusion, stupidities, and utter despair.

Now at this last meeting it was hard for me to grasp the fact that I had to say good-bye. What is this profession, where relationships must follow strict rules of *objectivity*? Dr. Hayes had broken those rules because he sincerely cared about my condition and had gone far beyond the call of duty, often sacrificing his own comfort and peace of mind. One winter night, when I had swallowed a bottle of pills along with a glass of wine, he answered a phone call even though it was after twelve. Because of Dr. Hayes I made it to the hospital emergency room in the nick of time.

In the office shelves full of large books lined the upper third of two walls. He sat by the desk in a revolving chair, and I took a seat on a small couch by the window. The beige mini-blinds were closed, but I could see traces of sunlight through the cracks. I set my backpack on the blue carpeted floor near my feet.

Doctor Hayes sat facing me. He had on a long-sleeved white shirt that looked bright and brand new. His tie, a shade of deep burgundy, stood out against that pure white background.

His fine hair had gotten thinner since the first appointment many years ago, but there was hardly any gray. He wore wire-rimmed glasses. Even though he was in his late sixties, his face showed few wrinkles.

His hands, relaxed, rested on the arms of the chair. He had long fingers, neatly groomed, and wore a faded gold wedding ring.

"I'll be getting a new office when I retire. They're painting it now. It'll be very nice."

He smiled and I noticed those few familiar crooked bottom teeth.

"That's great!" I said, trying to be enthusiastic. The word *retire* sounded so final.

But his retirement was well-earned. Once I had seen him walking to the hospital around 6:15 AM. And I'm sure he stayed until after five, most likely, past six. I couldn't remember him ever canceling an appointment.

Early in treatment I had tried to follow Dr. Hayes's suggestions along with taking the medications. But even so, my condition did not improve. Though I continued with appointments I soon went my own way, struggling with employment and relationships which amounted to failure after failure. I quit jobs repeatedly. I married and soon after, divorced. I felt the fool and, unfortunately, my life was one big validation that that was indeed the truth. All the while, Dr. Hayes patiently waited, offering psychiatric wisdom that often fell on deaf ears.

"Dr. Hayes adopted you," my mother once told me.

Over the years, whether I had acknowledged it or not, he was the life-line that kept me from homelessness, starvation, and total isolation.

◆ ◆ ◆

"I found a new psychiatrist for you," Dr. Hayes said, looking pleased. "First, I asked Dr. O'Neil if she is taking anyone new, but she said she doesn't see patients anymore. Her time is spent on speaking engagements in Europe and elsewhere, and on her writing. Next, I asked Dr. Thomas and she said that she only has one patient with the rest of her time spent in research. But I asked Dr. Gingerich and he said, yes, he would take you. Do you know who he is?"

I felt numb; my face frozen.

"No, I don't. I've never met him."

"Dr. Gingerich is an expert in the area of schizophrenia and pharmacological treatments. He is highly regarded in his field."

Still feeling numb, my mouth opened slightly to say, "Oh," but no sound came out.

"When you leave today you can set up your first appointment with him. Stop at the scheduling desk on your way out."

"Ok. Thank you for finding someone."

It was really kind of Dr. Hayes to go to all that trouble for me, asking various doctors, being turned down, until finally receiving a yes. At least now my future had a name: Dr. Gingerich. But would we get along? *Specializing in pharmacological treatments*—a possible pill pusher? Cold and calculating? *I* knew there was more to getting well than just popping a pill and Dr. Hayes knew that too. He wouldn't set me up with someone incompatible with my perspective. I had to trust Dr. Hayes; he knew what he was doing. But instinctively, I knew that it was ultimately all in God's hands and under His control. After all, I had left the decision up to Dr. Hayes as to who would be my new psychiatrist, and I believed God would work through him. Two months before when he asked my opinion, I had told him I didn't have a clue.

I had a present in my backpack for Dr. Hayes but was waiting for the right moment to give it to him. Suddenly I realized I'd probably never see him again. This, and the uncertainty of my future, caused me to draw a deep breath.

"I'm not going to live very long. I think . . . I think I'm going to die."

A startled look came over Dr. Hayes's face.

"I often have chest pains; it could be heart disease. I'm going to die soon . . . ."

In a very real sense my old life was going to pass away, my relationship with Dr. Hayes, perhaps, would end.

"There are tests to determine heart disease," he said. "You can talk to your general practitioner. Chest pains may also be symptoms of anxiety. Do you think you've been feeling anxiety?"

He had co-authored a text book on anxiety; he was considered an expert in the field.

"Maybe . . . I don't know. I feel like I'm going to die."

"What do you mean?" Dr. Hayes asked.

"This is the end, it's over. It's all over."

Doctor Hayes straightened in his chair; he then leaned forward and even though I avoided his eyes I felt them focused on my face. His voice became stern almost to the point of anger, yet I knew he was not angry.

"*Don't* give up," he said slowly, and after a slight pause, "Don't give up."

There was a moment of silence and then Dr. Hayes said more gently, "Are you going to continue with your writing projects?"

"Yes," I said, "I've written about my experiences with mental illness and the way I've been treated."

Encountering stigma had been a real test of faith for me. After I had left the cult and entered the world of the mental patient, I faced the inherent difficulties experienced by those with a psychiatric illness, especially prejudicial treatment from the larger community. I had felt rejection from virtually every segment of society: landlords, bus drivers, dentists, employers, store clerks, and relatives.

In another part of the world such as India, there is a caste system. The people lowest on this social ladder are the Untouchables. People of higher castes cross to the other side of the street to avoid coming near an Untouchable. They will tilt their heads downward and look to the side. If an Untouchable has taken the liberty to glance at their faces, they frown in disapproval. I had been treated this way on more than one occasion. Such is the position of the mentally ill in America: untouchable, subhuman, outcast.

Once, in my mid-thirties, I had volunteered at a domestic violence shelter only to be shunned by one of my co-workers. One day I overheard a conversation about me: "She's crazy you know! Disregard anything she says!"

FAREWELL

In the face of repeated rejection I often thought to myself, *Where is this God of love?*

"You could continue to write about how you found a relationship with God," Dr. Hayes said, "and elaborate on all that came about as a result of that relationship."

"I could tell about how God intervened in my life—if He had not done so, I'd be dead right now."

People with schizophrenia have a higher suicide rate compared with the general population. I had also heard that people with schizophrenia, on average, die about ten to fifteen years earlier than the normal population. I had smoked on and off for a while, never heavily, but enough to partially pollute my lungs. My love of fast food didn't help. McDonald's was a particular favorite. For much of my adult life I felt awful and wouldn't take care of myself.

Adding to the stigmatization and isolation I experienced was the problem of economic hardship. My numerous attempts at work had failed. Government programs were not sufficient for my basic needs. I fell into depression when I saw there was no way out of this life of poverty. Hopelessness set in with suicidal thoughts. Faith? What was faith? I found it hard to believe in a God who cares.

I continued to struggle with these questions throughout my adult life, attending church sporadically. Early in my thirties when I began to write, Dr. Hayes encouraged me to do more. I soon used writing to explore the meaning of life and shared my essays with Dr. Hayes. Now at our final meeting, he gave strong encouragement to for me to continue with my projects.

My projects in the past few years had reached broader dimensions not only because of the extensive exploratory reading in support of the work, but because when I was writing I did not feel alone. I felt the spirit of God guiding, nurturing, and inspiring me. Writing had helped me to feel emotionally stronger and more mentally stable. Now, being in the recovery process, I hoped to encourage others who suffered from depression or who were still drowning in a sea of symptoms. And maybe psychiatric professionals who read my work could gain some insight. I believed a life of faith could make all the difference in the world to someone who was wrestling with a death wish.

"It's been a long, hard struggle for you," Dr. Hayes said.

Suddenly, he grimaced and looked down toward the floor. It had not been easy for him either, putting up with me all these years. I'm sure he was remembering all the trials, not only of what I had gone through, but what I put him through as well.

"I haven't solved all my problems—"

"There will always be problems," Dr. Hayes said.

"God is on my side—or I'm on *God's side*."

"He is with you to give you direction."

I took Dr. Hayes's gift out of my backpack. It was wrapped in shiny silver paper and had a water fountain-style bow with sparkly silver strands flowing up from the center and falling down over the sides. Leaning forward, I handed it to him.

"Thank you," he said.

He carefully tore off the paper.

When it was unwrapped I said, "It's the best book I've ever read."

He looked at the title: *Miracles* by C.S. Lewis. The bridge and back cover were pink; the front was beige, brown, gray, and white with a photo of a child's hand cupping sea shells.

"Thank you," he said again as he flipped open a few front pages.

This book was important to me because I had experienced a miracle in my life and the recognition of the event for what it was had been my turning point. When I first became ill with schizophrenia in my early twenties, I fell into the turbulent abyss of psychosis.

Demonic voices bombarded me with obscenities and false accusations. This hellish nightmare continued for almost two years. In the midst of it all, one summer day a storm erupted with lightning and thunder. The downpour of rain became a voice and it spoke of light and hope: *"Believe in Jesus Christ and you'll be saved."*

I didn't listen.

Years passed, years of struggle and pain, until I took heed of the voice in the rain. The turning point came the year I nearly died in the suicide attempt. I later heard that the physicians didn't believe I'd make it through the night, and this was a jolt. Except for one good friend at this time my social isolation had reached the limit of my endurance. I was unable to cope with small daily frustrations and felt little motivation to write. It was as though I had reached the point of spiritual death. Then one day, as I sat at my typewriter in a spell of free association, I began typing the Lord's Prayer, and a door began to open. I decided to walk through.

I realized that in the most desperate of times God will reveal light to lead us out of the darkness. I had a choice to make and, finally, now in my early forties I decided to attend a church nearby and, eventually, I recommitted my life to Christ.

In Lewis's book I found support for my spiritual view of reality that not only validated my belief in the existence of God, but also explained the supernatural aspects of the human mind. My pleasure in giving Dr. Hayes this gift was immense.

We talked for a while about how recovery from mental illness doesn't necessarily mean reaching a specific goal, but that it occurs as a transitional process; that I may have a few setbacks, but I should remember that these problems would most likely be temporary. I said I believed I would always bounce back.

Then Dr. Hayes's eyes looked very serious and deep, became sad, even pained.

"I've taken care of you for . . . ."

He did not finish. His eyes became red and filled with tears. One fell down the side of his face, and he wiped it away.

I could not believe I'd never see him again, or rather I refused to believe it. He had been an important part of my life. The Bible says that God gives and God takes away. But it also says that God provides for all our needs. So who or what would fill the void? I had to trust and hope and wait. My future was not in my hands.

"It's time to say good-bye," Dr. Hayes said.

We both stood and he approached me. Bending down, he put his long arms around me and hugged. For a brief second my hands touched his back. This was rare; we had never touched one another except for an occasional handshake.

"I'll miss you," he said.

"I'll miss you, too," I said very softly.

But I wouldn't cry.

I bent down, picked up my backpack, and straightened.

"Good-bye."

"Good-bye," he said.

I walked out the door in a state of shock, holding back my tears. I felt so alone. My counselor would be gone. He had his own life, a life without patients, a life with family and friends. I had to grow up, learn how to be an adult, independent, yet dependent on the right people in right measure. Maybe the purpose of the relationship had been fulfilled and it was time to move on to what new plans the Almighty had in store.

Christ, while He walked the earth, lifted up the downtrodden, comforted the broken-hearted, and was a friend to those who felt excluded and unloved.

Over my lifetime my faith had been severely tested. But throughout these trials with help from God's people, I had been strengthened. Now I knew that my love for God would keep me going forward and I knew without a doubt, that as long as I had this bedrock of faith I could face whatever challenges lay ahead.

Dawn

Previously published in
You are entering your life: An Anthology of the PatientVoice Project
Edited by Austin Bunn and April Kopp (2008) 80.

Prompt: Write about something that has inspired you.

Instructor: Tim O'Sullivan

Once one has survived a near-death experience, everyday life is seen with a new perspective. My near-death experience occurred when I barely survived a suicide attempt back in my late thirties. Afterward, buried in a fog of doubt and confusion, I clawed my way into the light of life. Still, over a decade later, I experience rebirth in numerous ways on various occasions.

Recently, my friend advised: "Go outside in the early morning. Listen to the birds. What are they saying to you?"

So I went out. The morning, still dark from the cover of night, came alive with the delicate, yet mighty, chorus of birdsong. I walked about. A cardinal in a tree, one on a TV antenna. All around there were different kinds of birds merging notes and melodies, seemingly joyous, yet with a hint of melancholy. It then occurred to me that birds were not only singing in my neighborhood, but they were doing so all over the city, the countryside, the state, and the region. In fact, they sang anywhere the sun was rising, as it did all over the world. Such a thought captivated me in wonder and awe.

A neighbor opened her door, coffee in hand.

"Good morning," I called out.

"Good morning," she said.

When one has had a close encounter with death, afterwards, all that makes life worthwhile becomes more apparent. Now I don't take the singing of birds for granted. And I'll never forget one particular spring morning when the heavens poured down showers. I still heard one solitary bird somewhere out there in the rain. It sang, giving praise to its Maker. Undaunted. Loyal. So I thought to myself: let this be a lesson for me. Even while in the midst of life's storms. Sing.

Bibliography

Brand, P., and Philip Yancey. *Fearfully and Wonderfully Made*. Grand Rapids: Zondervan, 1980.
Buchanan, R., and W. Carpenter Jr. The Neuroanatomies of Schizophrenia. *Schizophrenia Bulletin* 23, no. 3 (1997) 367–72.
Dostoyevsky, Fyodor. *The Brothers Karamazov*. Project Gutenberg.
Fallot, Roger D. "The Place of Spirituality and Religion in Mental Health Services." *New Directions for Mental Health Services: Spirituality and Religion in Recovery from Mental Illness* 80 (1998) 3–12.
Grof, Stanislav. "Human Nature and the Nature of Reality: Conceptual Challenges from Consciousness Research." *Journal of Psychoactive Drugs* 30, no. 4 (1998) 343–57.
Hu, Guoqing et al. "Mid-Life Suicide: An Increasing Problem in U.S. Whites, 1999–2005." *Journal of Preventative Medicine* 35, no. 6 (December 2008) 589–93.
Jung, C. G. *Memories, Dreams, Reflections*. New York: Random House, 1963.
Kelsey, M. *The Other Side of Silence: A Guide to Christian Meditation*. New York: Paulist, 1976.
Keller, Timothy. *The Reason for God: Belief in an Age of Skepticism*. New York: Dutton, 2008.
Kierkegaard, Soren Aabye. *The Sickness Unto Death: A Christian Psychological Exposition for Upbuilding and Awakening*. Translated by Walter Lowrie. New Jersey: Princeton University Press, 1941.
King, Martin Luther Jr. *Letter from the Birmingham Jail*. San Francisco: HarperCollins. 1963, 1994.
Koenig, Harold G. et al. *Handbook of Religion and Health*, New York: Oxford University Press, 2001.
Luther, Martin. The *Presbyterian Hymnal: Hymns, Psalms, and Spiritual Songs*. Louisville: Westminster/John Knox, 1990.
McDowell, J. D., and T. Williams. *In Search of Certainty*, Wheaton: Tyndale House, 2003.
Moreland, J. P., and William Lane Craig. *Philosophical Foundations for a Christian Worldview*. Downers Grove: InterVarsity, 2003.
Mostert, Mark P. "Useless Eaters: Disability as a Genocidal Marker in Nazi Germany." *The Journal of Special Education* 36, no. 3 (2002) 155–168.

Bibliography

Murphy, Marcia A. *AIM Network Handbook: An Interview with the Rev Dr Timothy H. Little. Hope for Recovery.* (2016) https://www.hopeforrecovery.com/aim/.

———. "Before I Started to Serve." In *Different Members One Body: Welcoming the Diversity of Abilities in God's Family*, edited by Sharon Kutz-Mellem, 27–28. Louisville: Witherspoon, 1998.

———. "Christian Apologetics and Postmodernism: A Rebuttal." *Hope for Recovery.* (2009) https://www.hopeforrecovery.com/christian-apologetics-postmodernism-rebuttal/.

———. "[Coping With] The Meaning of Psychosis." *Psychiatric Rehabilitation Journal* 24, No. 2 (2000) 179–83.

———. "Dawn." In *You are entering your life: An Anthology of the Patient Voice Project*, edited by Austin Bunn and April Kopp, 80. Iowa City: The Patient Voice Project, The University of Iowa, 2008.

———. "Eugenics and People with Disabilities: The Roots of Societal Rejection, Neglect and Indifference." *Hope for Recovery* (2013). https://www.hopeforrecovery.com/eugenics-people-disabilities-roots-societal-rejection-neglect-indifference/.

———. "Farewell." In *You are entering your life: An Anthology of the Patient Voice Project*, edited by Austin Bunn and April Kopp, 30–36. Iowa City: The Patient Voice Project, The University of Iowa, 2008.

———. "First Person Account: Meaning in Psychoses." *Schizophrenia Bulletin* 23, no. 3 (1997) 541–43 by permission of Oxford University Press.

———. "God Cares: God is Close to the Brokenhearted." In, *More God, Less Psychiatric Illness: Devotions for Those in Recovery from Mental Illness*, edited by Marcia A. Murphy and Myrna Farraj, 1. Cedar Rapids: Eagle Book Bindery, 2017.

———. "God Loves the Outcasts." In, *More God, Less Psychiatric Illness: Devotions for Those in Recovery from Mental Illness*, edited by Marcia A. Murphy and Myrna Farraj, 2–3. Cedar Rapids: Eagle Book Bindery, 2017.

———. "Good Goes In—Good Comes Out." In, *More God, Less Psychiatric Illness: Devotions for Those in Recovery from Mental Illness*, edited by Marcia A. Murphy and Myrna Farraj, 18–19. Cedar Rapids: Eagle Book Bindery, 2017.

———. "Grand Rounds." *Schizophrenia Bulletin (Internet advance access May 4, 2006)* 33, no. 3 (2007) 657–60 by permission of Oxford University Press.

———. "How Do We Become Inspired?" In, *More God, Less Psychiatric Illness: Devotions for Those in Recovery from Mental Illness*, edited by Marcia A. Murphy and Myrna Farraj, 13. Cedar Rapids: Eagle Book Bindery, 2017.

———. "Letter to My Therapist." In *Fact, Fiction, and Little White Lies: The University Club Writers of Iowa City No. 3*, edited by Milli Gilbaugh et al., 115–17. Cedar Rapids: Eagle Book Bindery, 2014.

———. "Life Choices: What Do We Live For?" In, *More God, Less Psychiatric Illness: Devotions for Those in Recovery from Mental Illness*, edited by

Marcia A. Murphy and Myrna Farraj, 16. Cedar Rapids: Eagle Book Bindery, 2017.

———. "Our Actions Speak Louder Than Words." In, *More God, Less Psychiatric Illness: Devotions for Those in Recovery from Mental Illness*, edited by Marcia A. Murphy and Myrna Farraj, 18. Cedar Rapids: Eagle Book Bindery, 2017.

———. "Our Anger: What We Do with Our Own Rage." In, *More God, Less Psychiatric Illness: Devotions for Those in Recovery from Mental Illness*, edited by Marcia A. Murphy and Myrna Farraj, 5. Cedar Rapids: Eagle Book Bindery, 2017.

———. "Psychiatric Illness from the Religious Perspective." *Hope for Recovery*. (1997) https://www.hopeforrecovery.com/psychiatric-illness-religious-perspective/.

———. "Reflections." *Hope for Recovery*. (2013) https://www.hopeforrecovery.com/reflections/.

———. "Rejection, Stigma, and Hope." *Psychiatric Rehabilitation Journal* 22, No. 2 (1998) 191–94.

———. *Voices in the Rain: Meaning in Psychosis*. Cedar Rapids: Eagle Book Bindery, 2010. Reprint: Eugene: Wipf & Stock, 2018.

———. "What Does It Mean to Love God?" In, *More God, Less Psychiatric Illness: Devotions for Those in Recovery from Mental Illness*, edited by Marcia A. Murphy and Myrna Farraj, 17. Cedar Rapids: Eagle Book Bindery, 2017.

Newbigin, L. *The Gospel in a Pluralist Society*, Grand Rapids: Wm. B. Eerdmans, 1989.

PCusa.org. (2009) https://www.pcusa.org/.

Perry, John Weir. *The Far Side of Madness*. New Jersey: Prentice-Hall, 1974.

Pietikainen, Petteri. *Madness: A History*. Abingdon: Routledge, 2015.

Richards, P. Scott. and Allen E. Bergin. *A Spiritual Strategy for Counseling and Psychotherapy*. Washington, D. C.: American Psychological Association, 1997.

Robertson, D. B., ed. *Love and Justice: Selections from the Shorter Writings of Reinhold Niebuhr*. Philadelphia: Westminster, 1957.

Samples, K. R. *Without a Doubt: Answering the 20 Toughest Faith Questions*. Grand Rapids: Baker, 2004.

Shostrum, Brenda. *Spirituality and Health*. St. Andrew Presbyterian Church Adult Education Presentation. Iowa City, IA, 2008.

Sproul, R. C. *Defending Your Faith: An Introduction to Apologetics*. Wheaton: Crossway, 2003.

Stevens, J. "Anatomy of Schizophrenia Revisited," *Schizophrenia Bulletin* 23, no. 3 (1997) 373–83.

Sullivan, W. Patrick. "Recoiling, Regrouping, and Recovering: First-person Accounts of the Role of Spirituality in the Course of Serious Mental Illness." *New Directions for Mental Health Services: Spirituality and Religion in Recovery from Mental Illness* 80 (1998) 25–33.

Bibliography

Tamm, Maare E. "Models of Health and Disease." *British Journal of Medical Psychology* 66 (1993) 213-28.

Waldfogel, S. "Spirituality in Medicine." *Primary Care* 24, no. 4 (1997) 966.

Weil, Simone. "Human Personality," *La Table Ronde*. 1950 In *Selected Essays 1934-1943*, edited and translated by Richard Rees, 28. London: Oxford University Press, 1962.

Wikipedia, "Life of Christians in Science," Lines 1-45. https://en.wikipedia.org/wiki/List_of_Christians_in_science_and_technology.

Williams, T. "Reason and Faith." *Philosophy in the Middle Ages* [sound recording]. Chantilly: Teaching Company, 2007.

www.ingramcontent.com/pod-product-compliance
Lightning Source LLC
Chambersburg PA
CBHW070456090426
42735CB00012B/2569